USE WHAT YOU HAVE

How to take your *gifts* from potential to fulfill purpose

MOJISOLA OBAZUAYE

ISBN: 978-0-9956271-0-9

Published by Moj In Touch by Mojisola Obazuaye

A catalogue record for this book is available from the National Library.

Dedication

I dedicate this book to:

Those who have not allowed what they have been through to be barriers to who they can be by grace.

Everyone who has discovered their God-given gift and are using it fulfill God's purpose for their lives.

Praises for Use What You Have

Do you wake up dreading the day ahead and honestly wishing you do not have to go in to work?

Are you tired of the 9-5 or is it 5-10 work schedule?

Do you long to be more in control of your time?

Do you have passions you wish you had more time to pursue and then imagine getting paid for doing something you're passionate about? Won't that be icing on the cake?

If you can relate to any of the things above, why don't you get your copy of this book and allow Mojisola to take you on this amazing journey as she describes simple but practical steps to take your God-given gifts from latent potential to fruitful purpose.

I have been propelled, not just to sit on the fence and dream....but to make a difference in my generation...and to top it all, to get reimbursed doing what I enjoy. This for me defines FULFILLMENT.

Be like me and let this book drive you to positively use what you have.

Dr Abi Adenote
Internal Medicine Resident at Harlem hospital, NY.USA

I can honestly say this book is riveting. It is encouraging and thought provoking at the same time. Not only have I been blessed by it, I have been inspired to do so much more with myself and unlock all the potentials I have inside and fulfill purpose with them.

This book is one you cannot afford *not* to read. It will definitely lead you to discover yourself. It is a great read.

Thank you Mojisola, for sharing this masterpiece.

Rukayat Lasode
Co-Founder Kordlas Ltd

"90% of the population are stuck in a rut, running around in circles, trying to figure out what their gifts are. Others are busy discounting the gifts they already have due to fear and not making use of their gifts.

In this mind-blowing book; "Use What You Have", Mojisola shares sound tips and strategies on knowing, embracing, and honing your gifts. I love that she shared her own story of using her gifts to propel her life forward. This makes the book very relatable as I could identify with so many things she shared.

I highly recommend anyone who is still stuck or wants to know how they can use their gifts to make room for them to read this book. It will change your life...it changed mine!"

'Detola Amure,
Founder Super Working Mum + Author of Amazon Best Seller: Super Working Mum, Living and Loving Life to the fullest.

"Use What You Have" is a book that is filled with personal, practical, pragmatic, and powerful nuggets explaining how we can move our gifts from potential to purpose; achieving any and everything we set out to do. It exudes Mojisola's fantastic personality and passion; in a much deeper way than I see in her daily blog posts and videos. Reading this book instantly revolutionized my thinking and has particularly inspired and motivated me to revisit my dreams and rise to fulfill all I have conceived in my mind, obstacles notwithstanding.

I recommend this book; gender and age irrespective, to everyone who desires to fulfill purpose. It's high time everyone; young and old dropped every excuse and embrace destiny!

Mojisola , you have done so well with this and you are indeed a blessing to me and the world at large.

Sola Adesakin
Finance Coach, Motivational Speaker, and Author.

"Use What You Have"...now that is a book everyone should have especially in this fast moving world.

The book has blessed me richly as it has helped in opening my eyes to certain areas of my life that I have been battling with for a while. I have clarity on how to discover, embrace and own my gifts. Not only that, I am confident that with the practical steps in this book, I can take my gifts from just potential to fulfill God's purpose for my life.

This book is a must have for every household who wants more in life and wants to fulfill purpose.

Well done, Mojisola!

Olu Alewi
Quality Control Supervisor BBI solutions

Bravo! I like that the book is practical. The exercises at the end of each chapter help ensure that the reader takes decisive action. This is a good thing, because many times we get to listen to speakers or read books, get excited and forget everything the moment we walk out of the room or drop the book.

I also appreciate that Mojisola does not hold back anything in sharing her experiences from her journey. Apart from the learning points from the journey, it is encouraging to see how someone has been able to turn nothing into something substantial; from getting made redundant to turning this around for good. One of my greatest take aways' from the book is that you deserve to get paid for your gifts when you develop them. No apologies.

The bonus fashion tips toward the end also gave away the writers trait as a giver. Looking good is feeling good.

This is a book I would read over and over and recommend to anyone struggling with discovering and making the most of their gifts and talents.

Well done, Moji!

Mofolusade Sonaike
Founder Mumprenuer-Africa and Entrepreneurship Advocate

Feedback from Motivational Mondays as written on Mojisola Obazuaye's blog - www.mojintouch.com

Hi Moji, I just want to say thank you and God bless you. I almost gave up on me but looking and listening to you gave me the courage to start afresh. Now I see life positively because of you. Thank you!

-Danielle Dole (UK)

A book written by you would be so great! Your Monday motivation posts are always what I need to read at the specific moment I visit your blog. They inspire, encourage, and motivate me to go after my dreams. Thank you so much for the uplift always.

-Stella Asteria (Greece)

I always enjoy reading your motivation for Mondays. Love this week's motivation on having a positive mindset. I'm always telling my husband to watch his negative thoughts because of the tips you share on positive mindset. Thank you Moji.

-Jackie (Canada)

The words, the inspiration... I am wowed at all God is able to do when we stand still. Difficult as it may be to do...Lord, help me to be still. Mojisola, you are blessed among women. Thank you so much for this great motivation; I was blessed by it.

-Oluseyi Ashiru, Member of the John Maxwell team (Nigeria)

CONTENTS

ACKNOWLEDGEMENTS

I am thankful for inspiration from the Holy Spirit and wisdom from God to write this book. By my strength, I wouldn't consider writing a book but by grace, you gave me the urge to share. I give this book back to you my Father and Lord, take it and let your will be done in the life everyone who reads it.

To my wonderful husband, Efe Obazuaye, I celebrate and rejoice in your love always. You make me feel so beautiful. Thank you for being ever so supportive, mentoring me, making sacrifices to allow me the space and time to chase after my dreams and for pushing me to the direction I can't seem to find myself. You are indeed a part of my past, which has prepared me for now, and you will be a part of my very bright future by God's grace. I love you very dearly.

To our sons, Daniel-Ifedapo and Samuel-Ifelola, thank you for cheering me on. I am always very excited to hear your little voices say; Mummy how are you getting on? You couldn't wait for me to finish this book and here we are! My prayer for you is that all of the gifts God has blessed you with will never go to waste. Amen.

I celebrate the memory of my beloved Father for the love he gave to me as a child and for the solid foundation and preparation for life he taught me. I honour his memory for the love and help he shared with his influence to the needy, the poor, and particularly to the youth. Our lives have never been the same since you left us. Continue to rest in peace, dear Dad.

To my Mother to whom impossible is nothing, it is from your strength that I draw daily. Thank you for teaching me the importance of hard work and for instilling in me that though things may be tough, there will always be a way when we look up to God. Your prayers each time I get on the phone with you makes me stronger. You are the best Mum anyone could ever ask for. With long life I pray the good Lord Satisfies you. Amen.

To my sisters and brothers, I thank you for everything. I am grateful for the love you show me always.

A special thanks to my big Brother-in-law- Charles Obazuaye, I sincerely appreciate your person. Thank you Olasumbo Ayinde, I know I can always count on you. Special thanks to Kayode Fahm (RIP) for your humility to serve and for your kind advise on this book. Thank you, Claire, for all my blog photos. I thank you Detola Amure for your help, guidance, and mentoring throughout this book. You are a special vessel from God. Thank you, Leigh Ann Napier, for helping to edit and proofread this book.

I am thankful to my blog readers and clients from all around the world. Even though I say it all the time, I thank you so much for going on this amazing journey with me. It is because of you that I didn't stop writing, sharing, believing and continuing on the journey to fulfill purpose.

To my dear friends for all your love and support and to all the women in the entire support group I belong to, you all inspire me so much. Thank you. Thank you to all the members of the Gifted for a Purpose group for letting me serve you and for being a part of my world.

FOREWORD

"Having watched with interest the rise of Mojisola as a talented and beautiful woman from a close perspective as my sister-in-law, I wish I could re-title her book, "I am determined to succeed!"

Being asked to provide my perspective on her first foray into the world of writing is an honour and a privilege. Having been captivated by her several blogs on a range of subjects and in particular inspiration & empowerment, fashion and beauty, I don't think she realises that her big brother-in-law is a secret admirer of her work ethic and fitness to succeed. I have always admired her ability to grow words to capture her audience without undermining or sacrificing English as her preferred style of communication. I think there's a clear link between her faith and her communication style: gentleness, empathy and respect for others.

For me, what becomes clear throughout this book is two-fold: First, I, like many readers, admire Mojisola's creativity and ability to suffuse hard work and engage in complex diverse tasks with intelligence and belief. Her determination to articulate and share her beliefs and thus create sufficient followers is very evident in the book. Second, you also get a sense of someone who is in a hurry (positively, of course). Pace not panic - to make a real difference. The sense of purpose and sense of urgency is self-evident in the book. These leadership attributes help Mojisola to bring clarity and sense of encouragement for people like myself who passionately share the issues eloquently covered in the book.

Moji got the balance right in her mix of faith, beauty, and empowerment. The trilogy of body, soul, and mind is clear in the book. After all, empowerment is a body, soul, and mind thing! If you feel good about yourself, you'll find the inner strength and the Spartan courage to pursue greatness.

There's much more beneath the surface of Mojisola's beauty. As long as I have known her not too long to remember that I was the father of the groom (as the representative of my late father) when my brother married her in Lagos, Nigeria in 2004, she adores her faith and her family and her two boys in particular. She suffuses her faith with integrity and pragmatism. To find the time and motivation to write her first book whilst balancing a number of competing priorities in life is a testimony in itself. She possesses the same qualities HR professionals, like myself, tend to associate with successful leaders. She has the brain and steel to overcome any barriers or shatter any glass ceilings.

As a Manchester United supporter it hurts me to credit the great Arsenal manager, Arsene Wenger, with the mantra "possession with progression". This is true of Mojisola. She possesses the character to progress to the top sooner, because her fitness to succeed is unquestionable. Hence, I honestly believe this book is the beginning not the end of this young woman's foray into the world of social issues and personal development programmes. She is a good coach and mentor of talents. She is uniquely diverse, and this book has a few assertions readers will find self-evident.

Charles Obazuaye (CIPD)
Assistant Chief Executive/Director of Human Resources

FOREWORD

I have known Mojisola or "Ceci" as I love to spell my own version of her nickname for more than 27years. She has grown from a young ambitious beautiful girl into a hardworking, goal getting, truthful, compassionate and purpose driven woman. She is a shoulder to lean on in times of need. She's been like a big sis with her words of motivation and encouragement both in my personal life and business. She's probably the only one from my primary school days I'm still in touch with.

This book is extremely inspirational, eye opening, educative and spiritual. I am amazed at the depth of knowledge passed across in the entire book, and I must confess I found myself very emotional while reading to the point of tears streaming down my face even as I ask myself, 'what for' but all for joy to see how much effect the book has on the reader.

Aside from the book being very inspirational, it is also empowering. This book has the capacity to change an individual and make them the best version of themselves.

With this book, she has successfully been able to kill three birds with a stone by touching on our physical, psychological and spiritual lives. I believe strongly that this book will reconcile men with God. Indeed it is a God-given inspirational book everyone should read.

Well done Mojisola for obeying the leading to write this book.

Olasumbo Ayinde
Founder and CEO, Rennys Kitchen, Lagos.

INTRODUCTION

When I received the push from my Spirit Man that it was time to write this book, I was home alone, right in the middle of the kitchen doing some cleaning. As I cleaned, thoughts filled my mind and I immediately left the kitchen to put those thoughts down on my "thinking notepad". This is a hardcover notepad where I document random thoughts that come to my mind that I do not want to forget. Then later, I prayerfully take action to achieve those things.

The kitchen in our home is my second favourite part of our home. I spend a lot of time in there, first because I enjoy cooking (sometimes) and secondly, because I do some of my work in there. The natural light in there is perfect for filming my YouTube videos; I will tell you more about the videos in later chapters.

When I finished writing those thoughts down, I went back to cleaning. My heart was filled with joy for what God was doing in my life and where I believed He was taking me. With that smile on my face and my renewed excitement, I began to think deeply and my joy became fuller. With the joy in my heart, my mouth was filled with laughter like a girl who just fell in love. On that day, I was in love and in awe of what God was doing and I began to sing.

No wonder Maya Angelou says, "If you listen in the quietude of your heart, you just might hear the voice of God". On that day, it was quiet in the house and it was quiet in my heart; as I entered into deep thought, I heard the voice and the move of God indeed. I have never felt anything like that before; on that day, the voice of God came strongly on me. I felt I heard God clearly, right there in my kitchen.

As I continued to bubble with joy in my heart and praises in my mouth; I thought about how the scripture says that before we were formed, God knew us (Jeremiah 1:5). I wondered why God was laying this scripture on my heart? I almost instantly heard clearly that "What you are doing now is what you ought to have been doing a long time ago". When I heard this in my spirit, I remained still and listened attentively.

As I kept thinking and reflecting in my stillness, I thought about how everything seemed to be adding up for me. I reflected over a recent interview and was able to link my past to where I am. I thought deeply about what the future could look like for me if I followed through on the plans God has laid in my heart. I thought about how my past had unknowingly prepared me for where I am now. This was mind blowing to me in that moment!

Then, I also thought about one of my favorite lines that I like to quote every day; "Everything and anything is possible". This reminded me that no matter where we are from, what we have been through, what we are going through, who we are or how old we are, *anything and everything* is possible if only we are obedient in doing what God tells us to do.

That kitchen encounter with God is my inspiration for this book and so He led me to call this book, "Use What You Have". As the subtitle of the book says, this book will guide you on how to discover your God-given gifts, embrace them and take them from just a potential (wishful thinking) to fulfilling specific purpose for your life (getting results). I will talk more on potential and purpose in later a chapter.

The saying "use what you have" could be used in a very negative and derogatory way. My understanding of that line, especially in my University days, was that ladies slept with men for financial and material gain in return. Basically, such ladies used their bodies to get what they wanted...of course some men did too. That will still happen until the end of time but in THIS book, I bring a new meaning and positive energy to the phrase. The new meaning will give you clarity, understanding, and practical step-by-step guide on how to use your God-given gifts to fulfill specific purpose for your life. I will also share more on the title of the book, *"Use What You Have"* in the next chapter.

It is very important not to waste the gift or talent we have been blessed with because it is God's precious gift to us. What we do with the gift we have been given is our gift back to God.

Personally, since I started using my own gifts with the help of God, I have become more confident in the potentials that had been locked away inside of me; I am turning those potentials into purpose; I am living intentionally and deliberately; I have a deeper relationship with God because I am more confident in my personal work with him and I hear him speak to me; I have clarity for my life and no longer run around in circles; I have turned my gift into a "Career"; I inspire my sons to develop their gifts; I have become an authority in fashion and beauty and an encourager and mentor to many from all around the world; I write in the fashion & style column of many startups and still get invitations to write for more;

I am writing a book to become a published author; I have been featured on the Guardian; I have been invited to be a part of Youtube's Creators' Day at the Google headquarters in Dublin; I got the attention of Victoria Beckham who "favourited" a look book I created and I have been featured on the COVER of a Magazine amongst so many other things.

Did you notice I wrote, "cover" in capitals in the last paragraph? COVER! Being featured on the cover of a magazine doesn't happen to just anyone. It happens to the well-known, the famous…but grace brought it my way only because I took the possibility of being on the cover of a magazine into actually BEING on the cover of a magazine. In simple terms, when I started using the gifts that God gave me, I started achieving specific results I wouldn't have been able to if I didn't start using my gifts.

Why did I mention Victoria Beckham you may ask? She is one of the most respected people in the fashion industry today. For her to acknowledge a style look book I created meant that I was doing something right. Victoria's acknowledgement of my work would never have happened if I didn't start using my gift of creative writing and creative styling.

I wouldn't have been featured on the Guardian either if I didn't start using my gift of creative styling. That feature did not only bring me free publicity and a wider audience but it also made my work credible so that others started showing interest.

My greatest achievement so far is not that feature on the Guardian, the magazine cover, or the money I have made. Instead, it is the letter I got from a 17year old viewer of my YouTube Channel from West Virginia. She wrote to me to tell me because of my video titled "You Can't Give Up Now" that she was encouraged not to commit suicide. God used my video and this young lady was rescued from destruction. Since that email from her, I have been in her life, still praying with her and encouraging her. I have gotten more letters that were encouraging to me but that one's impact stands out to me most.

My hope with this book is to encourage someone else to step out and use their God-given gifts. Those "achievements" I mentioned since I started using my gifts and more, are what God has done for me. I know by my strength I couldn't have achieved any of the above. When we step out in faith using our gifts, He is there ready to partner with us.

Been successful and fulfilling our purpose is not limited to what we do or who we are professionally speaking. It is about truly pursuing what we love and doing those things diligently. Success isn't limited to a particular field or profession… Doctors or Nurses or Lawyers or Engineers.

Of course, it is okay to be a Doctor or a Lawyer or a Nurse or an Engineer or anything we want to be! In fact, I am a Microbiologist with a second degree in Industrial Biology and Bioinformatics myself with a career history of over 10 years in Banking and Financial services, Customer Service and HR. Getting a good education is very important but I caution you to not let your title or degree or profession stand in the way of you using the other gifts God has given you too. Trust God to pull it all together and leave nothing to waste.

I write this book to encourage that young man or woman who wants to be a Doctor and also has the gift of writing not to waste that gift. Also, to encourage that young girl whose desire is to be a Fashion Designer and has the gift of speaking not to waste that gift. And to that working professional to encourage her to also discover and use her gifts to fulfill her purpose.

The full picture and vision I have of this book is to encourage you to be who you want to be and also to look deep inside of you to see the gift you have and to use them to the fullest to fulfill God's purpose for you.

This book will awaken the Spirit Man of that unemployed man or woman, working young man and young woman, wives, mothers, stay-at-home mums and dads. May it unlock the potentials they have inside and glorify God in the process.

This book will encourage those who fear not being good enough or who lack confidence they could never be anything in life; inspiring them to look within and discover the gifts carried inside of them. When they do, they can't help but reach their fullest potential: God's purpose for them.

In this book, I also have a special note to dear women like me: I write this note to you dear woman that being a woman is special. It is very important to love yourself, use your gifts and be who you want to be. Even if you marry and have children, don't neglect using the gifts God has given you. Ask Him how you can use your gifts during each and every season of your life! He is faithful to guide you.

God has deposited at least one gift in each of us. In some people, God has deposited many gifts. There is not one person in this world that does not have a special gift! We all have received our gift by God that He will use it to work out our purpose. It could be the gift of speaking, writing, singing, styling, acting, playing an instrument, teaching, ministry, charity and on and on… it could be anything!

All of us have been blessed with at least one gift because the Bible says it is so in Romans 12 vs 7-8: we have different gifts according to grace given to us. If someone's gift is prophecy, let him use it in proportion to his faith; if it is serving, let him serve; if it is teaching, let him teach; if it is encouraging, let him encourage; if it is giving, let him give generously; if it is leading, let him lead with diligence; if it is showing mercy, let him do it cheerfully. These verses are the main inspiration and spiritual guide for this book and I will share more in a later chapter.

I recently listened to the TED Talk of a 10-year-old, Brandon Goldberg; the little piano man from Miami. I was blown away by how blessed and intelligent he is for a ten year old! And because of his intelligence, I wanted to see gifts from the eye of a child because I have children in this age group.

The young man confirmed my understanding of gifts and using them. He said in his TED Talk that "everyone has some 'instrument' inside of them and that they should find it because they never can tell where it will take them". It goes to show that no matter who you are or where you are from or how old you are, you have been blessed with a certain gift: one that is unique to you. You simply have to find it and use it so that God can be glorified through you.

When we discover our gifts and begin to use them, we can begin to get what we need for a fulfilled and purposeful life. We can change our stories for good, help others, make an impact in the world, and also make money! But most importantly, when we use our gifts, it is our own gift back to God and He will be glorified through us.

As you read this book, I pray God's guidance and clarity for you. I also encourage you to get a special note pad and pen to take notes. You could name it, "My Gift Book" or "My Purpose Book". There are pages on the back of this book you could use too if you don't have a notepad. I will lead you through exercises and this will be your place to keep it all together and have as a reference later.

With all my love and God's blessings,

Mojisola Obazuaye

Now, here's your first exercise.

- Are you ready to start using what you have?
- Are you ready to discover your God-given gifts and take them from just a potential to fulfill purpose? Is it a Yes or a No or a Not Sure? Write it down in your gift book and why you chose that answer.
- Whether it is a yes or a no or a not sure, this book will give you clarity as I use myself, our sons, and my darling husband as examples in this book.

CHAPTER 1

I FOUND MY STRENGTHS IN MY PAIN
(My Making Moment)

On the 12th August 2013, I had just returned home from work when my HR manager rang me and requested that I return to work at 9am the following day. I immediately questioned why I needed to return to work on my day off? I had other plans to spend time with my husband and he had taken time off work already.

On the other end of the phone, my HR manager said, don't worry; we will take care of it. I returned to work the next day and she and a few other HR team members broke the news to all of us that due to the economic downturn and after battling the decision back and forth, they have decided to make us all redundant.

I honestly didn't see it coming.

Did I feel my life was crumbling before my eyes? No I didn't. A lot of thoughts just filled my head with what was going to be the next step. My mind was running back and forth and with this and that. I was very unsettled. I took a deep breath in and then it was time to go home.

While so many colleagues of mine broke down crying and were visibly distraught, I was one of the few who were brave enough to "swallow" the announcement as if nothing had happened.

The only thought in my head was how to move on and where to go from there. What was I going to be doing and so on? I was wrestling with a lot of questions, as you would imagine of someone who just lost her job.

I drove one of my colleagues who wasn't handling the news well to her home. I then drove straight to my home and rang my husband who immediately came home after hearing my news. He looked me in the eye and held me tightly, told me to relax and then made me tea in my favourite giant mug. He had been asking me for a pedicure for the longest time and he was surprised when I announced to him that I would do his pedicure on the day I lost my job. What a thing to do to suppress the pain of losing my job?

When I announced to him I was going to do his pedicure, he said; Sisi, you just lost your job? I replied; it's okay, I will do your pedicure don't worry. I did his pedicure and we made food for us. While cooking we chatted, we caught up on things and laughed like never before and we ate. By the way, my father used to call me Sisi so it is an endearing nickname to me.

When I lost my job, I didn't have any business ideas at the time but I was always very interested in fashion. It is a passion of mine. I love to dress well and it is a priority to me to always look well put together at all times. I enjoy helping others look their best as well.

I had considered it a passion but hadn't done anything serious with it. I hadn't treated it as a gift or even a hobby at this time.

Of course I know a whole lot of people who know how to dress well but this to me is more than dressing well, it is indeed a gift. It just comes to me naturally. I visualize things in fashion, play them out in my mind and they always come out great in real life. Fashion is a passion that drives me; something that seems inborn, I never had to struggle to be good at it and it has always been so since I was way younger.

Another gift I discovered is writing. I figured out that I enjoyed writing a lot. Looking back, I recollected that I was writing since secondary school. I also have the gift of encouraging and it is one of the reasons for this book. I will tell you more about all of these in later chapters.

I was using just one of those gifts "somehow" but not the way I should. I have girlfriends who would call me for styling ideas, because fashion came to me naturally, I would go ahead to help them and they were always very happy with my work. I have always been the go to for all my family and friends styling needs.

Two weeks after I lost my job, I was forced to stay at home with pay while the organisation negotiated redundancy package and settlements. Two weeks passed and they didn't come up with something valuable so I continued staying at home.

In that two weeks, I had more time to do other things I loved like running, spending time with my family especially my husband and reading. I also had the time to pray more and write my prayer thoughts, requests, and thanksgiving down in my journal. Even though I was doing all those things before, losing my job allowed me more time to do more of what I enjoy doing.

After 4 weeks, we were all brought back to a fancy hotel to get our redundancy cheque. I got mine, headed straight to the bank and deposited the cheque in my savings account. Then I drove straight back home to continue sending out resumes.

Over the past four weeks, I had been applying for jobs and writing down ideas on what to do next but still wasn't sure. Even though I had money in my hands, things were still not clear to me. It was almost like I was in the dark on what to do next.

As uncertain as things were to me at that time, from my redundancy money, I paid my tithe; it was 10% of my total redundancy money. Humanly speaking, I battled paying any tithe from that money because I wasn't sure if I would get a job soon. I just wasn't willing to obey God's Word about tithing. Trust me, it is hard to give when you do not have so much and you are not sure of getting more.

Having said that, to a lot of people it would have been easy to pay that tithe. It was always easy for me but on that particular occasion, it was just very hard because of the fear of the unknown. All the same, I prayerfully obeyed and trusted God that all things work together for good for those that love God. In obedience, I showed that I love God and I believe that He will provide for me.

After paying my tithe, I felt a sense of relief. Although I was still worried about how everything would work out, somehow, I had the assurance that all will be well with me. I wasn't moved because I believed if I cried or get depressed over my job loss, it wouldn't change anything. Not that it didn't bother me, I just looked beyond it and focused on the things that make me really happy like my children who were very excited that I didn't have to go to work for now and my husband who was super supportive and encouraging. Most importantly, I focused my attention on God, the one who knows my end from my beginning.

I figured crying, feeling sorry for myself or being depressed would be a quick way to waste the "little money" I had in the bank. I knew if I was not careful, the money would be spent on medication to heel depression or junk to comfort myself whenever I felt down.

My assurance was just in God and his promises till the end. I also reminded myself daily of what Mathew 6 vs 27 says, "Can any of you by worrying add a single hour to your life?" Every time I think about those promises, I felt lifted even when I was down; I felt abundance even though I knew I might not get another pay cheque for a while.

As hard as this period was for me, I stayed focused on God. In that time I was also led straight to the story of Paul and Silas while meditating on how they waited on God in their time of trouble. They were expectant and not passive in their waiting.

A passive waiter would wait for a while and then give up while an expectant waiter would wait and hold on until something happens. The expectant waiters were Paul and Silas. While they waited, they praised and prayed and something extraordinary happened to them. They were loosened from all forms of shackles and were set free (Act 16 vs 25-26).

I started and continued praising and praying like Paul and Silas for God to show up for me and reveal what He wants me to do. And He did! All of a sudden, I got clarity on what to do. I got understanding from the book of Exodus 14 vs 15-16: Then the Lord said to Moses, "Why are you crying out to me? Tell the Israelites to move on. Verse 16; Raise your staff and stretch out your hand over the sea to divide the water so that the Israelites can go through the sea on dry ground.

From that reading, it was apparent that Moses needed God. Although God was with him, He didn't give him anything new at that particular moment. He instructed him to "use what he had" in his hand already for its intended purpose. He told Moses to stretch out the staff in his hand and that there will be a way for the Israelites to go through the sea. Moses obeyed and did exactly what God said, there was a way for the Israelites and God was glorified in the process.

Prayer must have a vital place in our lives, but there is also a place for action. Sometimes we know what to do, but we pray for more guidance as an excuse to postpone doing it. If we know what to do, then it is time to get moving.

Here came my "Moses moment"! It was time "to stop praying and to act" - to "use what I have in my hand". I was to create my own job for myself by using my God-given gifts; the job is going to make a way for me and through me, God will be glorified.

What I had in my hands or my "staff" at that moment are my gifts of creative styling, writing and encouraging. Following this leading, I wrote down exactly what I heard. Although I had clarity on what to create, I didn't know steps to take to create it but was willing and ready to learn. I was ready to learn and to do something new with myself. I was ready to leave my "comfort zone" which I knew wasn't going to be easy but I believed was doable with the help of God.

After this encounter with God, I started doing a lot of research and prayerfully, I began taking baby steps towards creating a brand new economy for myself since the reason why we were made redundant was a down turn in the economy. The economy I was led to create was a Blog to use my gifts of writing, styling and encouraging. To be able to reach audience visually, I created the YouTube Channel.

What is a Blog? A blog is simply a regularly updated website or webpage, typically run by an individual or a small group in a conversational or informal style.

Since I had my redundancy money in the bank, I invested that on the things I would need for my new job. I started by doing the research of the things I needed in that kind of field and wrote all of them down. After a thorough research and to ensure that I do not waste any of my limited cash, I bought everything I needed like a digital single lens reflex camera (DSLR); it is a camera for filming and photography. I bought a storage device (external storage device), I got some light for filming (artificial lighting) and the other things I needed to go on with my "new business".

After all that was done, I kept the remaining money in my savings account for rainy days and now it was time to go to work. I had all of the equipment but didn't know how to use them; I did more research, studied, consulted people, did trial and error and then I started working full time on the project.

To write a book was part of the vision God gave me when I waited on him in that dark period of my life. I wasn't sure of what the book was going to be about at the time but once I was sure, I obeyed and started writing.

Writing this book allows me to use my gift of writing and encouragement, which I had buried away for too long. Looking back, I am thankful that I lost my job at the time I did because without that, I wouldn't have been able to find this new direction and purpose I have found for my life. I am indeed grateful to God for such a time as that in my life as it has turned out to be my "making moment".

By the way, if you still do not understand the title of this book, it is from that reading I shared earlier in Exodus 14 vs 15-16 where God told Moses to "Use What He Had" in his hand. In this book, you will discover what you have just like I have, how they can make a way for you, how to use them to fulfill purpose for your life, and through you, God will be glorified.

As you can see in this chapter, I shared my own breaking moment, which has turned out to be a making moment for me with the help of God.

Please do the next exercise in your gift book:

- Have you ever had a breaking moment? What is it?
- What did you learn from it?
- Did you take advantage of what you learnt from it or did you let that breaking moment break you?

Listen, everything you go through in life is preparing you for a specific fulfilling season of your life. Pay attention to it but don't let it break you. Instead focus on God; prayerfully snap out of it and that situation or challenge or test will turn into a making moment or a testimony for you.

If you are broken or still down from your brokenness, I pray for uplift for you right now and strength and grace to move on from it. Amen.

CHAPTER 2

MY BLOG
WWW.MOJINTOUCH.COM
WAS BORN

I grew up with a Mum who doesn't believe in not working, especially for a woman. She always made it seem taboo to depend on a man for everything. Firstly, education was non-negotiable with my parents; you just have to get education. Secondly, she believes that at every point in time, you must be doing something with your hands be it paid employment, internship or training; the most important thing is that you have to be doing something at all times. She taught her children the ethics of working hard and she encouraged us to do better than she did. In simple words, she and my father raised us up to move mountains.

I particularly remembered as a child, I would feel like my mum was unfair. She would give me more than a hundred and one chores in a day, including opening her building material shop before I went to school in the morning. In the evening, I would make dinner for the whole family after homework and paid extra learning classes that we called "lesson".

I was also not allowed to go to school late. This meant I had to wake up early every day including Saturdays when I would spend the day assisting her in her shop: taking stock, attending to customers and doing some form of accounting for the week. We would clean the house on Sundays and then rest afterwards. I would spend most Sundays in my room reading one book or the other and I would paint my toenails because I was allowed. In the evening we would prepare for the next week. We would do some ironing, some cooking and every other thing that made the week run smoothly. That was my routine growing up.

I made my SSCE (leaving certification) results in one sitting and GCE (private leaving certification) in one sitting too. I got the awards from year one to year six in secondary school for the neatest student and I also bagged different awards for different subjects. I was also the Assistant Head Girl in my sixth year in secondary school (leaving cert year). I represented the school in debates, presentations, competitions and other events I was nominated to attend. I can boldly say that it was hard work that made me go straight to the University after secondary school.

All in all, my life was balanced, I didn't lack anything as a child but I learnt the importance of hard work, balanced life, and preparation for life. In simple terms, nothing was handed to me; I was taught to work hard for them. I wouldn't change anything because the foundation I had was solid. I am indeed thankful to my parents.

Little did I know that my Mum was preparing me to be a strong woman and wife someday who would appreciate work-life balance while also being who I wanted to be. Even though, I was a girl child, I was lucky to have parents who didn't see us lesser than the boys in the family. They just wanted all of us to do well irrespective of our gender and they made us know it was okay to be ambitious and to be who we wanted to be. And this is the reason why education in our home was non-negotiable; it was important so we could do whatever it is we wanted to do in life.

My Mum is my biggest inspiration and mentor; a generous and hardworking woman of class, grace and integrity who showed me by example that everything is possible. She modeled success for me as a woman. She has successfully ran her business for more than 40 years in a twin shop she bought for 5,000 Naira so many years ago when money had value; at that time, 5,000 Naira was a lot of money. Aside her building material business, she also has a Thermocool Franchise where she is a major dealer for her zone. She also has a few investment properties from which she makes revenue. This is an investment she made intentionally for her future and old age and as inheritance for us, the children.

I was really happy when I went home the last time and she told me she wanted to retire and wanted to hand things over to my siblings and myself. My prayer for her is for her to get rest after many years of working and I am thankful God has given her rest.

My father was an Electrical Contractor for different banks like Wema bank, Nigeria nationwide and a successful entrepreneur before his untimely death that changed our lives forever. He was passionate about empowering youths and he did everything in his power to make sure that all graduates that came his way got jobs;

this is one memory a lot of people have of him. He raised and trained so many distant relatives in business. He ensured that they were given foundation to do great things with their lives. I was a daddy's girl and I truly miss him.

All in all, I had blessed and hardworking parents who didn't throw things at us but taught us how to do things for ourselves. My sister and I would even follow my dad to his office in Ebute Metta-Lagos for holiday jobs! With the help of his secretary, I learnt basic office skills and ran errands in a professional way.

All of the things I learnt growing up inspired me to keep moving and doing something while I wait on recruiters to get back to me. I could never just sit at home and not do anything. This something was the Moj in Touch blog at www.mojintouch.com and my YouTube Channel at www.youtube.com/c/mojintouch. I am thankful for the training from my parents that keeps me moving forward!

Moj in Touch is a blog where I share fashion tips (body confidence and style coaching), beauty tips (skin care and make up), and motivation (inspiration on finding and fulfilling purpose).

I chose the name Moj in Touch for my blog because my name is Mojisola and I wanted to be in touch with who I was before I became a wife and mum; the young girl who became a lady and then a woman with a vision driven by purpose. I wanted to share my gift and that I would not let anything or any circumstance stop me. I wanted this to be an encouragement to other men and women to do the same.

I started writing on my new blog daily and I started creating videos once a week while I was waiting for a job to come. To me, the plan was for me to do this temporarily till I found a job and it will also be handy for me to fill out the gap in my CV which employers don't like to see. Unknown to me, God was taking me somewhere totally different and purposeful.

No response came from recruiters so I had to redo my strategy. I contacted a long-time friend who read and revised my CV. I soon realized I was wasting my gift when she told me she charged £150.00 for that service.

I paid a £150.00 for that service from the money I put away. Sounds ridiculous right? A lot of people thought so too but I did it. I got my first job afterwards. It was a fixed term contract. I made an investment in redoing my CV and it helped me fulfill a purpose. I will tell you more about the value of investing in yourself in later chapters.

In this new role I was conscious of the fact that it was a fixed term contract. I kept learning and working on how best to create content (create blogs and vlogs) with my current lifestyle working in a role in Human Resources at a multinational Pharmaceutical retail company and my family.

Meanwhile, even though I got a job with the help of the friend who helped revised my CV, I still couldn't get over how much I paid her for that service! That really inspired me to work hard at my new job and to develop my own gifts so that I could use them to the fullest. I was determined and inspired to take my gifts from just a potential to fulfilling my purpose.

I went back to the drawing board and created a new routine, which would consider all of my responsibilities and dreams: my family, my new job, and content creation (You Tube and Blog). And because I did a lot of "project management" while growing up, the experience was really handy for me to manage everything I had on my plate. I didn't have time to waste nor tolerate anything that would waste my time. I was laser focused and determined to do well especially on writing on my Blog.

At this stage, I am now settled in my new job and have also started creating content as planned. Even though it wasn't easy combining everything together, I kept growing and taking one step at a time. The more I blogged and vlogged, the more I wanted to do it, so I started thinking along the lines of making it a real career, not just a hobby anymore.

CHAPTER 3

HOW TO DISCOVER YOUR GIFT

Firstly, what is a gift?

A gift is something that has been willingly given to someone without payment; It is given free of charge. It can also be a natural ability, talent or strength.

Your gift is something you can do so much better and uniquely than the majority of others. It is something you are specially equipped and specifically chosen to do to fulfill purpose.

So how do you know your gift? Out of all the research I did for this book, this chapter took the longest because it is the reason for this book. I wanted to get it 100% right, and so I studied in depth for it. While studying, God directed me to the reading in 1 Corinthians 12. When I finished studying this passage of the bible, I was able to discover that to know your gifts, you should:

1. **Ask God to show you your gifts/strengths:**
   This simply means you pray for the revelation of your gift(s) to you. This may sound unrealistic or complicated. I struggled too to comprehend what my gifts were even though I knew them. It was not until I got quiet before God and really listened that I was able to hear what God was saying to me about my gifts and how exactly He wanted me to use them.

I used to think that to hear from God meant I would hear God speak from heaven and that I would hear his voice. No, it isn't so. It was revealed to me by paying close attention to the leading of the Holy Spirit. Having said that, God speaks to some of his children audibly. I pray for this kind of grace in my work with him.

See, every spiritual gift and every physical gift is the nature of God that you carry in you. And because God's gift is designed to find direction for your life, you will find great passion, joy and satisfaction in expressing it.

Passion is also an indicator to help you identify your gifts. Passion is truly something that drives you; it takes you where skills or knowledge couldn't possibly take you. Passion is the reason why you would wake up early to work on something; it is the reason why you stay up late at night to work and passion is the reason why you continue working even if you can't see the result of what you are working for yet.

I can boldly or confidently say that I am passionate about fashion. Why? This is because I do it naturally or effortlessly. It is one thing I do without getting tired. I find great satisfaction and fulfillment expressing it.

Another thing I am truly passionate about is encouragement. I found out that no matter how much I tried not to speak the words of encouragement even when I write fashion, I always end up writing or speaking them. Also, when people are in trouble, I always speak comforting words that help make them feel better. It comes naturally to me to do so.

When I studied 1 Corinthians 12 further, I got a clear understanding of where that passion to encourage came from; it was from verse 8 which says, "to one person, he gives the ability to give wise advice".

Please note that your gifts drive the passion in you. You just want to do what you love all the time, you are passionate about it, you talk about it and you don't get tired of working on it.

Now it is your turn to ask God. Grab your special notebook and ask him:

- What your gifts are and how does He want you to use them?
- Who does He want you to serve with your gifts?
- How can you use them to fulfill your purpose in your life and bring Him glory?

Take time to study 1 Corinthians chapter 12 and see what God will reveal to you about your gifts.

2. **Your friends and family will be able to tell you:**
   Ask them for feedback on what they notice you are naturally good at doing.

Remember I mentioned earlier that I was the go to for all my friends and family for fashion? They would commend the fashion advice I gave to them. When you do things and people start referring to how well you do it for them, pay attention to that thing and see what God is truly telling you about it. That could be your gift!

3. You will be able to recognize within yourself the things God has gifted in you:

Your gifts are the things that come to you naturally. You do them effortlessly and you are energized while doing them. Your gifts would normally give off clues. Your gift will cause you to react in a certain way in a given situation.

Spiritually for example, if your gift is that of shepherding, you will quickly come forward to care for a situation and make sure all is well. If your own gift is to pray, you will want to intercede through prayer on that situation or you may feel like gathering people together to pray about the situation. People with the gift of leadership will come forward to say; we have to look for a solution for this problem and ensure they are solved.

In the physical for example, if styling people comes naturally to you, that may be your gift. If decorating or doing interior decoration feels effortless to you, that may be your gift. If speaking, acting, singing, painting, mentoring, cooking, teaching, counseling, writing, or any other thing comes to you naturally, that may be your gift.

Think of things that come naturally and those things you do and receive compliments from others. Your gifts give you clues by your reaction and action in a given situation. To discover your gifts, pay attention to what you like to do that is stress free for you. It could be anything from writing fiction to make-up artistry to mentoring to speaking etc.

Currently as parents, we are praying to God for him to help us discover our sons' gifts. We want to help them build on their gifts even now while they are still young. We pay close attention to what they like and what they don't. We talk to them about and ask them what they like and how we can help them develop those interests.

For example, we discovered our older son Daniel, is very good with his hands. He is playing the guitar by himself with the help of online tutorials and videos. We also noticed that he loves fixing broken gadgets especially computers around the house. Initially we thought he is taking after Daddy (Efe, my husband) because he is an Engineer, but we discovered he is truly passionate about fixing things. Because of his interest, we have also decided that he goes to a secondary school where they have an option of computer and coding.

Daniel would take the time to read up tech news, watch repair videos and all things related to programming and computers. He would upgrade computers; do repairs with the help of Daddy. Now he does repairs by himself effortlessly. Recently, he fixed the church's PC by himself. To help him develop playing his guitar, my husband and I have decided to enroll him for proper guitar lessons and buy him an upgraded guitar so he can improve on it.

Even though the interest of children may change, investing in his gifts would still help him at some stage in his life. It could be something that could help him stand out or showcase him later.

We observed some clues that helped us discover that Daniel enjoyed working with his hands. Daniel would reach for his guitar and play on it when he has nothing to do; he would play on it while waiting for us to get out of the house if we are going out as a family. He wakes us up with the sound of the guitar; he plays after his homework etc. He basically plays it all the time because he enjoys it. As for repairs and fixing things, he is also very enthusiastic about coming forward to say I will do it.

Aside from using his hands, Daniel is also very compassionate; he cares about people. Recently, the Principle of his school called me to ask if Daniel could help with an Autistic child during break period. They figured that Daniel was drawn to the child and would care for her during their lunch break whenever they played in the yard. For the whole of the school year, he was helping out with the child during break. The Principal said, "the child feels calm and relaxes around Daniel".

As for our younger son Sammy, he started reading at a very young age, as young as 2.5years. We noticed that he was always fascinated with books. Daddy (Efe, my husband) was the one that first noticed this when he came back home from Nigeria. He then started spending time with him with flash cards and before we knew it, Sammy was reading long and short sentences. Before Sammy got into junior infants, he was reading, spelling correctly and writing perfectly. His teacher would call me and ask how I managed to get him to learn to read, spell, and write at a very young age. I told her we would spend time nurturing his gift and teaching him.

When Sammy was in 2nd class, his teacher made a special connection with him because of how clever she thought Sammy was. She would give him extra work in school, take time after school to teach him new things, and it went on and on throughout his second year in primary school. We believe he was favoured and we are thankful for that divine connection with his teacher.

As Sammy is getting older, his interests haven't changed; he is more interested in books, news, newspapers, weather reports and he is always very interested in all things academics. He also likes to narrate news, weather and sports… especially to Daddy who listens to him more.

We have prayerfully paid attention to our sons' interests and we are helping them develop and build on them. We are also very intentional about not forcing what they do not like on them. Provided what they are doing is good, we are going to support their gifts and the potentials they have till those potentials become purpose.

Grab your "gift book" and ask yourself:

- Do I know my gifts and am I using them?
- What are 5 steps I can take to know my gifts and how can I begin to use them?

Don't rush; this could take you more time than you think. Have you done so? Brilliant! Now keep that "gift book" handy for your next exercise.

CHAPTER 4

TRY YOUR GIFT OUT

If you still do not know what your gift is or what your gifts are, it is possible that you may have more than one gift. One of the ways you can truly figure out and be sure about what your gifts are is to start by volunteering in your local community, church or an internship to try out your gift. Once you start out using what you think may be your gift, you will begin to discern if that is your gift.

Like I said earlier in chapter 1, I have the gift of encouragement. The gift of encouragement is not too different from the gift of teaching. I do know that I am not a teacher but each time I am called to teach in my local assembly, I find out that I do teach well. I have also done presentation in form of teaching on so many occasions in live events I have been invited to speak at.

You may be wondering how I could speak well too even though I said I am not a teacher or I don't think I have been gifted to teach. I figured you can write encouraging words and you can also speak them. And because I do better in writing encouraging words than speaking them, I always have to write my teaching down first, study it and then speak on it if I need to. And sometimes I don't write them; I just speak as I get utterance and I do well.

Since I have been speaking or teaching, I have also figured that you can build on or develop your gifts or what you are good at. The reason is because the more I speak, the better I have become and most of the practicing I did was by making videos where I speak words of encouragements. Recently, I looked back at my very old videos and the ones I have done lately, I discovered that in the newer ones, I spoke more confidently, boldly and my pace of speaking was not as slow as it was when I first started. What this tells me is that I have built on or developed my gift of speaking. I will share more on developing or building on your gift in later chapters.

Looking through my personal self-development and study notebook, I figured out that every topic I have talked about, spoken, taught or written about are all words of encouragement. Please note that you will always be drawn towards the direction of your gifts.

Thankfully, anytime I teach, I always get feedback that I did well. I do not ask people, but I have had people personally call me to say *well done, you did really well, we were blessed by your teaching, or we were inspired by it.* I get this feedback also on my blog and videos from readers from all over the world; I shared some of such comments at the beginning of this book.

When you try your gifts out, you will be able to discern if that is your gift. If it is truly your gift, you will be naturally drawn to it and you won't struggle at it. You would want to continue doing that particular thing. For example, writing is one of my gifts and I have developed it. I noticed that if I don't write in a couple of days, I start to feel incomplete. When I go back to writing, I feel some kind of fulfillment and joy, simply because writing is something I truly enjoy.

Now it is time to grab your gift notebook again!

- **Have you discovered what you are good at?**
- **When you tried it out, did it come to you naturally and you didn't struggle at it?**

I hope you have discovered your gifts or are getting closer to knowing what you are good at.

Now for another exercise:

- Write down one simple step you want to take to develop that gift. It could be by taking a short-term training, volunteering or internship.

Well done for writing it down! I can see you are ready to take your gifts from just a potential to fulfilling your purpose. Please ensure to keep your "gift book" handy for your next exercise.

CHAPTER 5

DON'T BE AFRAID, THERE WILL BE A WAY

Once you have discovered your gift, there may be times when the fear of not knowing what to do can make you feel like not following through on using what you have. This is why I asked you to write down just one way you intend to start developing your gift in the last exercise. If you haven't done it, please go back and do it now.

In chapter 1, I mentioned that after I bought all the things I needed for my blogging business, I didn't know how to do it but was willing to learn. So, if you ever feel like you don't know what to do, don't worry and don't be afraid. Just be ready to leave your comfort zone. In simple terms, you need to be ready to work hard at it.

If you ever feel afraid or the fear of not following through comes to your mind, the first thing to do is to go back to God. He was the one that blessed you with the gift, so He will help you. I like to say this a lot, "a little prayer helps and a lot of prayers help a lot". So pray and be willing to learn.

God will not come down from heaven to help you but when you ask him to help you, He will direct you to people who can help you or send them your way. He will begin to show you what to do, how to do it and when to do what.

To be able to enjoy all of those benefits, you must have a relationship with God. Know him and let him know you. Well, he knows you by name even before you were born but God wants you to have a relationship with him. When you do, he hears you when you call.

GET ON YOUR KNEES

The one thing a lot of us fail to do is pray. Yes, a lot of us don't. When trouble comes, when we are afraid, when things are not going the way we have planned, or when we want to start using our gifts, a lot of us fail to pray instead we continue to run around in circles or from pillar to pole.

Some of us talk to other people about our problems or plans while some of us keep them inside. The most important person to talk to when you are about to do anything is talk to God. Luke 18 v 1 says: "Men always ought to pray and not to faint". Prayer works, pray!

No matter what the situation is, you must talk to God. I said in the previous chapter that He would send helpers your way if you ask him. His promise is if you ask, He shall give to you according to Matthew 7:7. So learn to talk to God in prayers.

In Chapter one, I shared that when I was in the dark about what to do after I lost my job, I praised and prayed to God. Then I got clarity and I figured out what to do. It was then that I started using my gifts. Prayer works so please pray in whatever situation you are in today.

Praying does not have to be only on your knees. You can pray while standing, sitting, driving, and the good news is that you can pray anywhere! God just wants you to have that communication with Him always and not only when you need Him.

CALL THEM TO COME

I have heard and seen a lot of motivational speakers, coaches and mentors use the word affirmation. Affirmation simply means a process of pronouncement or assurance. For you to be able to achieve anything you cannot see, you must also learn to confess them. When you begin to confess things, you motivate yourself to go and achieve them. You will achieve them because you believe them already and the strength to go work on or for them will be supernaturally given to you.

As it is written, I have made you a father of many nations in the presence of Him whom He believed-God, who gives life to the dead, and calls those things which do not exist as though they did" (Romans 4:17)

See the B part of that scripture above, call the things you want to come, believe them even as you work for them, and you will achieve them. Yes, you must be ready to work because there is no short cut to success.

Now do this simple exercise:

Write down an affirmation to yourself in that "gift book":

Say with me, "God has given me supernatural strength to build on my gifts and all the help I need to take my gifts from potential to fulfill purpose are sent to me". Amen.

Well done, you did great!

YOU NEED THE HELP OF OTHERS

I know for sure that I am a "smart cookie". I try hard at everything and I believe I can do everything I'm called to do with God's help. Isn't that what the Bible says? Yes, we can do all things through Christ who strengthens us!

Even though God promised that we can do ALL things, we still need the help of other people because we cannot do everything on our own. You need the help of other people who do the same thing as you, you need the help of people who know the things you don't know so you can have time to do the things you are truly passionate about and the ones you do effortlessly. Things you do effortlessly are your gifts!

When you let others help you, you grow quicker. You add your helper's knowledge to yours, which makes you better as a person because you learn from them. You will also have someone to look up to and to hold you accountable.

I remember it was when I started sending out questions to people I admired very much that I began getting a lot of clues as to what to do and how to do them. They were the helpers God sent to me

GET A MENTOR

Sam Adeyemi, Preacher and Author says we all need mentors but a mentor does not have to be someone you pay but someone you look up to. Yes, you need a mentor for you to be able to quicken your ability to take your potential into purpose. Having a mentor is important even if you are naturally driven, self-disciplined, and motivated.

When you are starting out anything, be it a project, business, or using your gifts, you need someone who can guide you, direct you, influence you, encourage you, pray for and with you, and someone who can help you set realistic goals and hold you responsible till you achieve them. We all need individual help from someone we can look up to. We all need a mentor. I am thankful for the mentors in my life.

When I was starting out my Blog and YouTube, I mentioned I didn't know what to do but was willing to learn. I reached out to others who were doing what I was going to start. One was Khadija -Peak Mill on YouTube who now does YouTube full time and has a successful business. The other was Stella - Jadore Fashion who has been blogging for more than 8 years and has built a reputable brand from blogging. I wrote to them with my questions and they came back to me with some great advice that went a long way for me. Their advice gave me hope that if I tried and worked hard and by grace, I would do well. Both ladies inspire me so much.

Along that line, God sent me another helper; Stella from Fashion and Style Police who also quit her full time job to go pro-blogging. She inspires me very much too.

So don't let fear of not knowing what to do paralyse your potential of using your gift to fulfill your purpose. It may take time but it will surely happen. If you don't know anything, please ask, it makes a lot of difference.

GROUP HELP

We are in a technology age where everyone, everything, and anything are online. Online, we also have so many groups. For example, on Facebook, there are a lot of groups created by different heads of businesses, leaders and mentors. Look for a group that shares helpful and beneficial tips on what you do or what you want to start doing; you will be surprised at what you can learn from them.

In a group, you find different people from different walks of life. When they share their ideas, suggestions, and opinions and you join all of that with what you already know, you will be filled with so much. The more you know, the better you will be.

With the help of God, I was able to create one of such groups; The Power Dressers Group where I share Fashion, Beauty Tips and Motivation with women from all over the world.

The group power is that you necessarily do not have to see the people in your group. Some of them you may never meet in your life time but the wealth of knowledge you could take away from them are money can't buy experience.

Group help could be online, in your local community, your church, or a group of women/men who share common goal in your area or niche etc. So join a group that could help you. Be careful however not to join a group of time wasters. Be careful not to join a group that will give you a headache, focus on problems instead of solutions, and waste your time.

Now for your exercise, grab your gift book!

- Do you think you need a mentor or group help?
- Can you think of anyone right now who is of great influence to you or someone who can mentor you? Write their names down in your "gift book". Prayerfully approach them and ask if they can mentor you to take your gift from just a potential to fulfill purpose.
- If you think you would benefit from group help, do your research and join one that will help you.

Keep your "gift book" handy for the next exercise and don't forget, let your mentor be someone who can help you develop your gift further not one who will distract you and change your vision.

CHAPTER 6

BE READY TO WORK

You may have heard the saying, no pain-no gain. For you to be able to achieve anything, you must be willing to work for it. If you work with professional coaches or mentors, they will tell you that you still have to do the work even though you pay them. No, they won't do the work for you. Coaches and Mentors only encourage you, inspire you, and teach you strategies to DIY. DIY simply means, "Do It Yourself"

See this reading; the soul of the sluggard craves and gets nothing, while the soul of the diligent is richly supplied (Proverbs 13:4). You must be ready to go from craving something, to planning to do that thing, and then begin to do the thing. This simply means you must go from wishful thinking to taking action. It is when you begin to take action that you can get the results you desire. Wishful thinking will not get you anywhere. Wishful thinking will never turn your potential to a purpose. You must take action toward your goals.

DENY YOURSELF

Denying yourself is not as bad as it sounds. It means you must be ready to leave your comfort zone. For example, if you used to sleep for 8 hours at night, you must be willing to lose some sleep. You must be willing to rise earlier than you used to or sleep later than you would normally do so that you could get some work done on learning how to develop your gifts. You may have to read, train, and learn to develop your gift.

If you love to watch television or play video games, you must be willing to deny yourself of enjoying those things you love for a time. Denying yourself is not hard by grace. It simply means you are stepping away from those things that take your time or waste your time in order to develop your gifts. These times wasters are things that are preventing you from using what you have. You need to identify where you waste time and make a commitment to avoid those things while you are developing your gift. It gets easier as you start to see progress.

To be able to use what you have to fulfill purpose, you must be willing to make the sacrifice of not buying what you love/like. I am a shoe lover and I love the very good ones. In my Introduction, I talked about how I invested most of my redundancy money on the things that will benefit my blogging and vloging business. That was denying myself. The urge came to buy at least one pair of "good shoes" but I didn't because I quickly reminded myself that shoes don't appreciate in value. However the investments you make in yourself or for your future can never depreciate in value. Even if you lose "everything" in life, the investments you make in yourself can never be taken away.

Grab your "gift book" and do this simple exercise.

- What do you really love and that you know you waste your time doing?
- What are 2 ways you can deny yourself of those things while you work on developing your gift? Take your time to do this.

Well done, you are doing great.

WHEN ARE YOU PRODUCTIVE?

On my time right now, it is 4:16 am so this means I am writing in the early hours of the morning. I mentioned in the sub chapter; "deny yourself" above that you must be able to deny yourself of some sleep. It is not enough to deny yourself or just be busy for being busy; the most important thing is to be productive even as you deny yourself.

To be able to be productive, take note of when you are most productive. Is it in the daytime, nighttime, or the early hours of the morning? For someone like me, I like to wake up very early, earlier before my children and husband, to get some work done or late in the night after I have tucked everyone to bed including my husband.

So I encourage you to know when you are most productive. The time you function best, concentrate best, and the time you are most focused to get some work done. Try experimenting with the different times for working on sharpening your gifts and see when you are most productive. The most important thing is to have something to show for denying yourself and being productive during whatever time of day you choose to work.

The thing about getting some work done when you are most productive is that at that time, you could do so much more than you would compared to when there are distractions. Also, using your productive hours means that nobody would know about it but when you show your results, they will find out and begin to wonder how did you do it? That is fun to share with others that they really do have time they didn't believe they had. If you are willing to make the sacrifice, deny yourself of your luxury time wasters, and work hard, you can do anything.

Now do this simple exercise in your "gift book".

- When is your productive period? Is it in the day, in the night, or in the early hours of the morning?
- Write down goals you want to achieve in those productive hours of yours. Take your time to think about it. Set realistic goals but work hard at them.

You are doing great and you are setting yourself up for success. Well done!

INVEST IN YOUR SELF

Investing in myself is something I struggled with a lot but now I know better. And because I now know better, I am doing better. Not investing in yourself is very dangerous because if you lose every material or physical blessing you have, you will be left with nothing. It will be a shame to lose everything and not to have something left inside.

One of my greatest inspiration and mentor is Efe, my husband. He pushes me into the way I can't seem to find myself. Although initially, I thought he was always too hard on me. But now I know it is because he wants me do more so that I can achieve more. Now I am doing more and achieving more and it feels really great.

Allow me share with you some self-development that rescued my husband. A couple of years ago, my husband got a professional trainer in a particular Information Technology field (IT) who trained him for some professional certifications and exams he wanted to do. He paid this trainer heavily because he learnt privately. He had money but didn't have the time or the skill but was willing to move from the better place he was to the best place he could be. For that reason, he got a trainer who would come after business hours to teach him. He learnt a lot by investing time and money in himself. He also had to study hard so he could have a result to show for what he was doing.

Unfortunately at some stage, he had serious problem with his business due to the carelessness of someone else; he lost a lot of money and his investments. When everything was gone, he was left with all the training and skills he acquired from that trainer. With all of those skills, although it took a while, he went back to college (university) to retrain and got back into that field where he had acquired skills. Today he is an Engineer with one of the Nation's Telecommunications Company. He is good at his work and his skills are missed anytime he is not around. A lot of times, he is called to work because they are stuck on what to do. I am proud of him and I am thankful to God for giving him the inspiration to believe in self-development.

Also not investing in yourself doubles your pile of work and it means you have to source information on and about everything. Doing all of that takes time and a lot of effort too. You may not also arrive at the result you desire which could be painful and discouraging if you didn't get result after all the work you put in.

You must be willing to pay in order to gain. Investing in yourself does not mean you have to spend money though. It could be simple things like:

1. Going back to school to take a free course to learn something new or acquire a new skill.
2. Watching free online resources to learn something new. I gave an example of how our son, Daniel is using free online tutorials to learn the guitar in chapter 3.
3. Using your local library to borrow books you do not have access to or books you cannot afford.

I have also heard of the saying that you do not appreciate what you do not pay for. There is truth in that too. When you invest money in a course or training, you may take it more seriously and work even harder because there is an investment at stake. I encourage you to pay for developing yourself if you can afford them, it will benefit you in so many ways at some point.

Sometimes, you may not be able to afford some kind of investments but you must be willing to make the sacrifice to get them in order to reach your goals faster and gain momentum.

Here are some examples:

1. Paying to develop your gifts through learning
2. Paying to be mentored or coached
3. Attending seminars and retreats
4. Buying books

In my case, even though fashion and beauty comes to me naturally, I had to spend money to learn Image Consultancy so I could be an authority in that field. Always do your best to invest in your gifts and whatever you are passionate about.

For up to 4 years plus, I learnt so much on beauty and skin care by working as an Independent Beauty Consultant with a reputable make up brand so I could speak, write, and teach beauty and skincare boldly. Today, I do that and I enjoy it so very much. So I could learn more on make up, I spent hours and hours on learning make-up tips and tricks by watching professionals and working for free on clients. I also spent hours and hours watching and learning fashion and everything fashion. That is what I do; I made time to learn and study the things I needed to learn.

From my experience, when people see that you are truly passionate about something, they will offer things to help you. Maybe a book they have they think you would like or they will let you know about a resource they think would interest you. I have received so many gifts that have truly helped me in going far in my field of work and business. You can only receive such gifts when you start using your gifts and when people start seeing that you are truly passionate and committed to what you do.

One example goes back to when our son, Daniel showed he was serious about learning to play the guitar. We had a desire to upgrade his guitar because he has self-taught himself by using online tutorials and he is playing quite well. We wanted to be obedient to this conviction God laid on our hearts to send him to professional guitar lessons.

My husband and I went away to London for a couple of days and the children were staying with a friend. Daniel didn't bring his guitar with him but as soon as they settled in, he saw a guitar in the room where he was going to be staying. He took the guitar and started playing; when this friend of ours saw that he was playing really well, she offered him the guitar, which was almost new! Although we were going to buy him a new guitar, now we didn't have to buy him one anymore, we didn't need to because his gift made a way for him. He was only in that house for a day and already his gift was noticed. His gift and his hard work at working to learn by himself had made a way for him.

Whatever it is you have to do to invest in yourself, you must be willing to do the work because it will come back to you and make a way for you. All investments come back whether good or bad. I say invest in good things especially to develop your gifts, invest in things that will benefit and enrich your life. Just like our son's gift made a way for him just in a short period of time when he was in a new place, your gift could make a way for you if only you truly develop it. It wasn't until Moses used what he had in his hand that God made a way for the Israelites (Exodus 14 vs 15). When you start using what you have, God will make a way for you so He can be glorified through you.

Now grab your notebook:

- What is one thing you think you should invest in learning to help you develop your gift?
- Write down an action plan to achieve it.

Well done, you are doing great!

HOLD ON, CHANGE WILL COME

A lot of times when we venture into something new, be it a business we started after losing our jobs or one we started because we want to use our gifts, we expect some kind of results, growth, or change in our circumstance to come quickly. When the changes we desire don't come quickly, we can begin to feel discouraged, angry, oppressed, or intimidated…and sometimes we quit or at least really want to quit.

Please be patient and also know that change takes time, it takes patience, it takes persistence, it takes perseverance and it takes a lot of faith.

START WITH POSITIVE THINKING

For as he thinks in his heart, so is he; Proverbs 23:7

Your mindset as you go into anything new really matters. If you go into anything with the mindset of failure, you are most likely to fail. If you go into anything like a success, even if the road is rocky, you will be a success.

Which would you rather have? Success or failure? It is critical that you start with a positive mindset. Your mindset must be set on a high and not a low. You must be able to convince yourself that you will do well with God helping you. (Philippians 4:13)

You must be able to assure yourself that you will stand out even if there are more than a million people doing the same thing as you. From your reassurance to yourself, your faith is strengthened and the physical strength you need is boosted to do what you have to do.

Even though your mindset has to be positive, you shouldn't over think what you hope to achieve and never set unrealistic goals. Unrealistic goals could make you feel overwhelmed and discouraged when results don't come as fast as you would like. Over thinking on the other hand causes anxiety. Both are bad for productivity and growth. Learn to live in the moment. Living in the moment brings joyful living.

HOW DO I STAY POSITIVE THEN?

You only attract what you focus on. If you focus all your energy on negatives, you will attract negative things and vice versa.

Take your eyes off any other thing, people and what they have to say or do and focus it on God. You cannot waste space in your mind with negative thoughts. You must make room for what God's Word says is true and refuse to be discouraged by negativity.

Let God be your strength in times of weakness, your joy in times of sadness, and your comforter when you need comfort because He is the one who teaches you and can give the wisdom to make wealth. While wealth may be monetary to a whole lot of people, being wealthy is truly achieving or fulfilling God's purpose for your life.

STAY AWAY FROM NEGATIVITY & NEGATIVE PEOPLE

Unfortunately, there will always be negative energy around. The best thing you can do for yourself is to remove yourself from that negative area. If you have to leave the place, leave. It will be worth it for your mental health and productivity.

Negativity or negative energy could also be a relationship you are in. If you are in a relationship that is toxic or one that brings you negative vibes, you owe it to yourself to excuse yourself. When you look back, you will be glad you did. I am not talking about marriage relationship now. I am talking about casual relationships. But I am not encouraging you to stay in a physically or emotionally abusive relationship either.

The simple logic is this; when you are in any environment that is negative or where people are lacking in zeal to achieve specific goals or where people are not living intentionally, it is always hard to be productive. Stay away from negative situations so you can be focused and be productive. If you are not surrounded by positive people in your life then seek them out by reading about them, watching videos of inspiring people, or joining masterminds full of positive people who are taking action toward their goals and dreams.

Now do this simple exercise.

- Do you think you need to let go of any relationship that is distracting you from using your gifts to the fullest potential?
- Write the person involved down and weigh your options. Do you think you will be better off with or without that person? Now is the time to let go so you can focus on you and the things that are very important to you.

If you are bold enough, let them know that at the moment, you are busy getting yourself together and focusing on you and that should be it. No hanging out together, no long telephone conversations, and no chatting online for too long. Know that this is something you need to do for yourself to become the person God created you to be. The sacrifice will be worth it. Now that you have decided to let go, there is no excuse not to do well at using your gifts. You can do it.

DON'T SHARE YOUR BIG DREAMS WITH SMALL MINDED PEOPLE

The small-minded people are the ones who remind you of how things cannot be done. They see negative in all situations. They remind you of how many people have failed in what you are about to start and so much more. They will poison your dreams if you drink the negativity they are pouring out. Don't drink it! Take note of such people and never share anything with them. They will discourage you and create fear in your mind.

What will fear do? Fear is a joy killer. It will not only steal your joy, it will prevent you from using what you have to fulfill purpose. Fear brings stressful living and fear paralyses your ability to do or be anything. Do not be afraid or allow yourself to be. The bible reading in 2nd Timothy 1 vs 7 says; For God hath not given us the spirit of fear; but of power, and of love, and of a sound mind.

The God inside of you is strong and mighty and so are you because God is in you; and everything God can do, you can do with His help. You are limitless; don't limit yourself and the ability you have to use your gifts to the fullest and to fulfill your purpose. I pray any fear in you be silenced right now in Jesus mighty name. Amen.

SURROUND YOUR SELF WITH LIKE-MINDED PEOPLE

Jim Rohn says you are an average of the five people you spend time with.

When you spend time with people and you feel worthless, tired, or your energy feels drained, then you may be hanging out with the wrong people.

On the other hand when you spend time with people who make you feel lifted, energetic, motivated, inspired, and encouraged, then you are in the midst of the right people.

The people you mingle with will rub off on you and will determine whether you will remain in the right state of mind to use what you have. You owe it to yourself to stay and surround yourself with people who share the same goals, vision, and aspirations as you who are willing to dream big and work hard.

In Chapter 6, I mentioned that one of the ways you can invest in yourself is for you to get mentored by a coach. Although one of the strategies mentors and coaches use to sell their business to you is that they use the word "you can afford it".

Yes, for you to be able to invest in yourself, you must be willing to make the sacrifice by denying yourself of the luxury you normally could afford. If you are one who can't truly afford a coach, look for ways to stay in the midst of people who can empower you, motivate you and guide you. Although you may not be paying for that kind of service, you will still be able to learn from them.

Also, even if you have a Coach or a Mentor, let your true mentor and coach be God Himself. He is the King of Kings and the Lords of Lords. He is the all-knowing and He is the coach to all coaches. He is the best coach that can mentor you and He is always waiting there for you to come to Him. Connect with him just like you connect with friends on Social Media. The connection you make with God is the most important connection you could ever make. It is a connection that can never fail.

Have a personal relationship with the Father and let his fear be in your heart and He will reveal all of those things those coaches do not know to you. The secret of the Lord is to those who fear him and He will make them know his covenant (Psalm 25:14)

Do this simple exercise:

Do you have a personal relationship with the Father? If you don't but would like to encounter what it feels like to know him, please say this simple prayer with me:

"Father, I know that I have broken your laws and my sins have separated me from you. I am truly sorry, and now I want to turn away from my past sinful life toward you. Please forgive me, and help me avoid sinning again. I believe that your son, Jesus Christ died for my sins, was resurrected from the dead, is alive, and hears my prayer. I invite Jesus to become the Lord of my life, to rule and reign in my heart from this day forward. Please send your Holy Spirit to help me obey You, and to do Your will for the rest of my life. In Jesus' name I pray. Amen"

Wow, Congratulations, you have been saved! Now continue to seek more about the Father and join a Bible believing church to fellowship. Do not forget to take your personal relationship with God seriously. That is more important.

BE PATIENT

One of my favourite lines to say is that "God rewards hard work". My children are quiet familiar with me saying it too; whenever they feel like they are doing so much more than their peers, I quickly remind them that God rewards hard work.

You see when you work hard at anything you will eventually get results. Getting result in your own case may be different from other people's case. Be patient and your own result will come. Ecclesiastes 3:1-8 talks about there being a time for everything. Be patient, the time to get your own results will come.

Don't forget, you are writing your own story. Face your work and write your story the way you want it to be with the help of God.

Patience now is a virtue everyone must have. But if we hope for what we do not see, we wait for it with patience (Romans 8:25). I said earlier that for you to achieve anything you must have faith and for you to be able to receive what you have faith to receive or achieve, you must be patient. So be patient, your time will come.

ALLOW YOURSELF TO STAND OUT

No matter who you are, where you are from, what you've been through, or what you are going through and no matter what your gift is, you can stand out. For you to succeed at anything, you may have to go through trials, and you may even have to strive but you can make it and will stand out only if you let yourself with the help of God.

One of the ways to stand out is by doing your own work in your own way. Do it diligently, do it cheerfully, do it with all your heart and show up every day even if you don't want to or even if you are discouraged. When people see you today, and tomorrow and the next day, they will never forget you. You have to position yourself in such a way that you will stand out and be remembered.

Always remember that the potential you carry inside are unique to you; they are uncommon. No one else has them exactly like you even if you do the same thing or share the same passion. You are still unique in how God has made you and matched you with your life experiences.

To stand out, you should always aim and learn to do your own thing in your own way without trying to be what you are not or like anyone else. Do things in an original and undiluted form; according to that reading I shared in the introduction of this book in Roman 12 vs 6, you have been blessed with a unique gift; now aim to do all things in your own unique way. If you write, do it in your own way and so also if you serve, teach, sell etc, do everything in your own unique way as God leads you.

It is when you do things in your own unique way that you can stand out from others, discover yourself more, live in your purpose and fulfill your purpose. When you do things like other people, you will always be a replica of that person and you will always be in their shadow.

Continuity, consistency, and communication with God are keys to make you stand out. No matter how many people do what you do, no matter how many people have failed before you, you can stand out.

Allow me share just one reason why I know you could stand out. When I got invited to be a cover girl, in the letter they wrote to me, they said "we do know that there are a lot of Fashion Bloggers from all around the world but out of all of them, we decided that you are the one we want on the cover of the magazine because you are a woman of CLASS and GRACE".

I was blown away, humbled and I am still very thankful because in the Fashion blogging world, you have women and men from all works of life who wear and model the best outfits; couture, designer labels and much more but they chose me. The reason is because I positioned myself in a graceful and classy way and no matter what I always do things in my own unique way and it was apparent to them and to others.

No matter how small you think you are or how little is what you do, do it graciously, with class, and in your own unique way and you will stand out by grace.   You can do it, allow yourself.

PAY THE PRICE NOW OR START OVER

It is very easy to give up or quit when we do not get the results we crave or want on time.

You know the saying; quitters don't win and winners don't quit. That saying is true because if you quit, you will not get the results you want anyway. Why not persevere provided you are doing the right thing.

If you think you may need help or are struggling to get results, search out a mentor. They will be able to help and guide you. Pray to God to send your own destiny helper as I call them. God has a mentor and coaches he can send your way; He will do it for you.

I remember when I started blogging on www.mojintouch.com, I met a lot of amazing ladies who would visit my blog when they have the time. I would visit theirs too as time allowed. The idea is to show support and read their blogs and learn from them too.

Along the way, some of them I was quite familiar with stopped blogging. I sent personal messages to a few of them to ask them what was going on and to see if all is well with them. A few of them came back to me to say, blogging isn't for them, some said it takes too much time and some just were not ready to put in the work which is necessary to achieve any goals.

Unlike traditional blogging; blogging these days is very rewarding if you can do the job because it opens a lot of opportunities including monetary. You can also turn your blog into a real business. I have seen a lot of successful businesses that started out as blogs. Blogging could be a stepping-stone to greater things only if you can put in the work.

However, blogging involves a lot of writing depending on what you blog about. If you are not truly gifted at writing or you do not have a vision to take your blog from just a potential to a specific purpose, you will "chicken out" because it involves serious but doable work if you are truly passionate about what you do.

Why did these "Blogger friends" of mine stop blogging you may be wondering? I will share that with you in the next chapter.

CHAPTER 7

IS THIS GIFT YOURS?

I shared how to discover your gifts in Chapter 3 and one of the ways I shared was that your gift would normally come naturally or effortlessly to you. I also said that your gift will give you clues by how you respond in certain circumstances.

If you struggle with what you consider your gifts; then those may not be your gifts. There are no two ways about it. God doesn't give you gifts you will struggle with. You may have to put in the work to get what you want but you will not have to struggle if truly that is your gift. Your gift is supposed to come naturally to you and you are supposed to use your gifts effortlessly. You do not strive to use your gifts; you thrive while using your gifts.

THAT IS NOT YOUR GIFT

I mentioned that your God-given gift would ideally come naturally or effortlessly to you. It is something you do uniquely than others. A lot of people struggle with what they consider their gifts because they are doing the wrong thing.

For example, I mentioned that I met a few people who had blogs but stopped blogging because they find it really difficult to write or are just not committed to blogging.

Sometimes life happens and would force us to stop doing what we truly love and are passionate about. A lot of times, people go into things, they ought not to go into because they see other people doing that particular thing and those people are doing well at it or are thriving at it.

If you go into anything just because some other people are doing it,

1. You will find it difficult to do.
2. You will struggle and strive and may not achieve anything out of it.
3. You will be frustrated, disappointed, and angry.
4. You will eventually give up.
5. You would have wasted your time.

GO BACK TO THE BASICS

Now you have realized you are using a gift that is not yours or you are doing what you are not supposed to be doing. It is time to go back to the 3 suggestions I made in discovering your gifts in chapter 3. The good thing is that it is never too late to ask God for anything. God answers when we call, He is our Father. He doesn't expect us to do everything perfectly.

To truly know your gift, I encourage you to focus on my number 1 suggestion in chapter 3: Ask God for the revelation of your gift. Once you know your gifts, you will never struggle to use it and with it, you can fulfill your purpose in life.

IT IS YOUR GIFT, DON'T LET ANYONE CHANGE IT

One of the reasons why I believe it is important to be sure of your gift is that when you are sure, nobody can change it for you. It is YOURS.

When you start using your gift and things are not going as fast as you want them to, it is possible to feel discouraged; in most cases you talk to people about it.

Yes, it is okay to speak to people about it especially if you have a Mentor or a Coach, speak to them. Now, this is the tricky part; be very careful so people don't talk you out of God's initial plan, purpose, or vision for your dreams and gifts.

Let me give you an example, when I first started blogging and nothing positive seem to be happening. I began to doubt if I could go anywhere with it; this was just a doubt which could happen to anyone. I spoke with someone who quickly told me to try blogging gossip. In her words, she said, "Gossip blog would "blow up" on time". "Blow up" simply means "making it big". The person also gave me an example of people who have done really well doing gossip blogs. It sounded really appealing I must confess.

When I dropped the phone after speaking to this person, I realized I was going away from God's plan for me if I changed my fashion, beauty and inspiration blog to a gossip blog. That wasn't my vision and initial plan when I started using my gift of writing and styling. My vision is to be known for Fashion, Beauty and Motivation, so I stuck with it and was determined to work hard with the help of God to get to where I want to be. I am still not where I really want to be now but I am thankful I am not where I was. With God on my side, I will get there.

So I tell you, once you are sure of your gifts, visions and where you want to go with it, be careful so no one talks you out of it. If you let that happen, you may derail and then have to go back to what your gift is or what God has told you to do in the first place. This would have amounted to a waste of time and effort. You can't buy time back so don't waste it.

YOU DON'T NEED THE VALIDATION OF OTHERS

A wise one once said, "the best people to learn from are the ones who have made mistakes so you don't repeat the mistake they have made". Sincerely, this is the wisest thing anyone should do.

I pay attention to a lot of people who are way older than me. I do this because I believe they have more life experiences than me. When such people speak, I keep quiet and I listen attentively because I am learning from their experience. If they have ever made any mistakes, I learn from their mistakes and prayerfully make up my mind not to make that kind of mistakes whether in marriage, in career, in finances, and in all areas of life in general.

This is not relevant to gifts but I will share because it is an example of learning from someone older. Out of so many other things, one thing I learnt from my mother is never to buy actual size clothing when I started having children. When I was pregnant with my first child, I went to the shops and bought at least two sizes bigger than a new baby's actual size. When I had my baby, the clothes were a little big on him but not ridiculously big but they lasted longer. And because I did that, I saved so much money on baby clothing. Up till today, I still use the same trick, buy at least two sizes bigger than my children and I don't have to buy clothes all the time because they grow into the bigger sizes I buy for them.

Surprisingly, this simple trick was made for me because I have very tall children and they don't fit into clothes recommended for their age. Presently, my 11 year old wears an adult's size small and my 9 year old wears an adult's size extra small. I will continue to use this trick and save money. Of course, I will be teaching them the same thing for their own future family.

Another thing I learnt from my mother is to always put money away. She always says, "if you don't put money away, when a need arises, you will always have to go and borrow". She would say unfortunately, you might not get to borrow when you need money. I hope someday, I can write a book on "how to never be broke".

Some older friends and I were chatting one day and they talked about how they allowed what other people thought about their vision to talk them out of it. And because these people talked them out of their vision, they stopped doing anything to pursue it. Automatically a conceived vision became an aborted one; they altogether stopped thinking about it and did nothing about it. I felt pain for them when they said so. I felt pained because waiting for other people's validation destroyed the "fruit" they could have had.

Listen, there will always be people who will never believe in what you are doing; there will be people who would never see what you see, there will be people who will not see what you are worth or what you can offer and there will be people whose dreams would never tally with yours. While all of that is okay, it is **<u>NOT</u>** okay for you to wait for anybody's validation before you go ahead to do what God has laid on your heart to do. In that reading in Exodus 14 vs 15(a) I shared earlier, God said to Moses, "Why are you crying out to me"? This same thing is applicable to any vision God may have laid in your heart. Don't wait for anyone to validate it for you, just keep moving once God says it is time to go.

In the first place, these people whose validation you are waiting for were not there when God gave you your vision and or gift. They weren't there. Why wait for them to validate it for you? It is unnecessary.

Instead of waiting on people to validate your dreams, go ahead and continue doing what you have to do. When you get results, they will have to believe in what you are up to.

As I read through this page, I can confidently say that on my YouTube channel I have had more than 128,000 views approx. and on my blog, I have had more than 1.2million views from all over the world since I started. What this means is that those amount of people have come in contact with my work even though I may never meet them in person till I leave this world. However because they have had a contact with my work, it is possible that I have impacted, influenced, or inspired them. Isn't that great?! Imagine if I was waiting for anyone to validate what God has laid on my heart to do? It would be a waste of time and I would have missed out on reaching all of those people.

The only approval you need in your life is that of God. When God tells you to go, just go and when he says stop, please stop. Waiting on others to validate what you do or seeking their approval will slow you down in life and in getting where you want to be.

Sometimes your gift may not be popular like a lot of other people's gift. Does this mean you should derail from it because it is not popular? No, you shouldn't. Go ahead and stick with developing your own gift and use it to the fullest. Whatever you do, let your goal be to take your potential to God and let him work it out in His purpose for you. Your aim is to let your results speak for themselves and not what anybody thinks or has to say. Go for it, you do not need the validation of others.

Now do this simple exercise.

- Write down one thing in your "gift book" anyone has tried to talk you out of doing.
- Now write down one way you can rekindle your love for that thing.
- Think of ways you can get results in doing that thing.

Well, done, you are on the right path.

74

CHAPTER 8

GIFTS ARE NOT ENOUGH
(Potential to Purpose)

Yes, you now know your gift and you are using it to be who you want to be. Well done, you have come a long way. Now is time for you to take your gift to the next level by learning how to use it professionally.

In whatever you use your gift to do, you want to position yourself as the best. There may be a million other people doing what you are doing so you want to be on top of your game.

IMPORTANT NOTE!

In the next chapter and the following ones, I will be sharing serious self–development tips, moneymaking tips and potential-to-purpose tips with you.

Time to really pay attention!

BE ON TOP OF YOUR GAME

The world is highly competitive and moving really fast. When it comes to gifts, you have to be on top of your game. Back in the day, you had to go to a physical school to learn something new. In this modern technology age, you can learn anything, anywhere, and at any time. It is the best time to learn! You can even do it from your smart phone.

The things you know last year may not be enough for the following year. Be willing to learn more and do more so you can achieve more with your gift.

Personal development is a life-long process so it is necessary for you to have a personal vision and mission statement just like any brand or business. It is important to regularly assess your talent, skill sets, and qualities. Frequently assess your aims in life and set goals so as to be able to realize and maximize the purpose you could achieve from your potentials.

Personal development is the best gift you can give to yourself. You must also be ready to learn new things, new skills and new ways of doing things to be able to be competitive in your niche. No matter how small the investment you make in yourself, it will surely come back to you. Investing in yourself in the area of your gifts will never be a waste.

Even though it is important to learn more so you can know more, focus on you and don't let your attention be on what every other person is achieving. That is important so you do not feel under pressure or feel discouraged.

Always remember that you are not in a competition with anyone. Let your plan be to be better than who you were in your past with the help of God and not to be better than other people. This is how you can truly win in life and bring glory to God. I say again, focus on you because you are unique.

Now grab your "gift book" and do this simple exercise.

- Write down a new skill you think you can learn to help your gift go further.
- Write down an action plan to achieve that new skill you think you should learn.

Well done! Don't forget to follow through.

CHAPTER 9

YOUR PAST SHAPES YOUR FUTURE

We cannot change the past, that is certain but we can build the future we want with God's help and by constantly working towards our goals.

You see, I have a science background, my first and second degree. Looking back, I discovered I have always loved the Arts. By loving the Arts, I mean I have always loved fashion, beauty and creativity in general. Also, I have been writing since I was in secondary school. I didn't consider myself a writer until I started getting paid for writing for other websites, blogs, and businesses though.

Let's go back a little to illustrate how your past shapes your future: I joined the Press club in my secondary school and was made the secretary to the press. I did all the writing and would put out an article a week on the pressboard.

Fast forward to when I got to the University, I also joined the Press club. It was more challenging in the University because I had to write an article a day for the pressboard. What that meant was that I had to combine writing an article a day with lectures, studying, and every other thing that came with being a university undergraduate.

Remember in chapter 3, I shared that one way to know your gift is when others draw attention to it or talk to you about it? My then Pastor, Gbade Ogunlana would send me complimentary notes on how well I looked and how well I put my clothes together. He kind of encouraged me then to have some kind of "business". Unknown to me, he was basically drawing my attention to my gift; not that I wasn't a serious person at that point in time, I just didn't pause to meditate on his words of encouragement. I am convinced that this was why I sensed in my spirit like I said in the introduction that I heard God say clearly that what I am doing now, I ought to have been doing a long time ago.

In the University, I also had the opportunity to sell and style clothes. You may be wondering how I did that? It wasn't long after Gbade Ogunlana drew my attention to my gift that a Masters degree student, Tolu saw me in the faculty and approached me while standing in the midst of my friends; she pulled me aside and said, "I like the way you dress a lot, would you like to help me sell some of the clothes I bring from Dubia". I didn't know this lady so I asked for time to think about it. I saw her precisely three days after she first asked me and I said yes, I would help. She would hand over the clothes to me at a particular price and I would sell to make profit. And because I did well, she would also give me bonuses/tips.

My passion for styling took over while I was just casually selling. I would give suggestions on what to wear and with what to the Ladies who were buying and then the news spread. This helped me to make so much money at the time. I was a young undergraduate but was making money while doing something I loved. The offer that lady gave me was another pointer to my gift of styling.

Everybody knew me, supported me and cheered me on. I was nominated as the best-dressed student in my final year. Even though I came in as the runner up, I was still really pleased that someone noticed.

Also one benefit for being a member of the press was that I got accommodation throughout my stay in the University (except for my 2nd year because my application was dropped in late). I stayed with my dear Friend Olubunmi Fajinmi-Alewi that year. She is still one of my best friends till date.

What am I saying? I am saying that the things I did in my past pointed me to my gifts and molded or prepared me for my present and the future I can picture by faith. Still following through my gift of writing and styling. Currently, I write and contribute to a few fashion blogs and websites and I do it so effortlessly. I have also had the chance to style different women from different walks of life. Most importantly, I have a Blog and YouTube Channel I am so proud of because I am able to reach many people from all around the world.

In simple words, I have managed to take my gift of writing and creative styling from just a hobby to fulfill a specific purpose for my life; I have turned what I have into a "career". And because of the motivation series I have on my YouTube Channel, I have also had the opportunity to speak to an audience of more than hundred on more than two occasions. I am confident that by faith, I will achieve so much more and impact so many more lives and people from all over the world.

I had to take you through all that because unknown to me, my past has prepared me for now and now is preparing me for the future I see or picture by faith. You can do so much more than I have done because I believe you have so much potential inside of you. Do what you can to make that potential turn into purpose. It will be a shame for them to remain a potential forever. You can turn them into purpose so God can be praised through you.

As you go on in life, in whatever capacity you serve or whatever it is you do, ensure to pay close attention to what you are doing. Reflect on your past as much as you can but don't dwell in it. See how what you did before can give clue to your present and then your future.

Also, pay attention to everything that may have happened to you or the things you may be going through now, they are necessary and are preparing you for your future. With God's help, you can link your past to your present and this can help guide you to a fulfilled and productive future.

Whether you had a terrible past or a smooth one, once you make up your mind to go for something, go for it whole-heartedly without any negotiations or doubt in your mind. All you have to do is to make up your mind on what you want to do, how you can begin to do it, and how you can be a success at it.

I recently read a quote on a friend's Facebook page and it said; "So often, we pretend we have made a decision, when what we've really done is signed up to try until it gets too uncomfortable".

In simple words, that quote means; when you start using your gifts, you must make up your mind that no matter what happens, be it distractions or a little set back, that you won't give up. The good news is, the more work you put into whatever you do, the more results you will get out of it. Why don't you just do the work so you can get the result?

Grab your "gift book" and do this simple exercise.

- What is one thing you were truly passionate about in your past?
- Write down an action plan that can help you rekindle your love for that thing.
- How can you use the same thing to help serve others and better your life now and in your future?

Wow, well done. You are doing so great.

CHAPTER 10

YOUR GIFT WILL MAKE A WAY FOR YOU

One of my inspirations for writing this book is one of my Pastors, Emmanuel Ilori. He is an Author of 2 great books.

When I got the push in my spirit that it was time to write this book, I approached him casually and asked him a few questions I had about publishing, he gave me a few tips and he immediately held my hands to say a prayer of agreement with me. From time to time, he would call me to ask how I was doing on the book. I am grateful for his time and encouragement.

When he was having the launch of his second book, he had booked a photographer to take photos at the event. Unfortunately, the photographer rang him to say he couldn't attend on the day so his wife reached out to me to see if I could help. She reached out because she knows I do some kind of filming.

When she asked me for this favour, I knew deep down my heart that I wasn't good at photography but I am good at filming. Even though I knew deep down that I was likely to mess up on the day, I said yes I could help. You may be wondering why did I say yes? I said yes because the mindset to always have is that you can do all things through Christ that strengthens you. And of course as a man thinks so he is. I believed I could do it and so I said yes even though I became afraid as soon as I said yes.

Another reason to always have the mindset of "you can do it" even though you can't is because one of the most successful entrepreneurs in the UK and founder of Virgin groups (which comprises of 400 companies) Sir Richard Charles Nicholas Branson, once said; "If you get offered a job or a role, even though you don't know what you do, take on the role and then figure out what and how to do the job later." It means, if you truly put your mind to do something, you can do it.

On the day I was called to help with photographing that book launch, I started researching photography, how to take at least reasonably good photos. At the end of day 2, I managed to figure out how to take presentable photos.

On the day of the book launch I was very nervous because I was worried the pictures may not turn out good. I hoped and prayed that the photos turned out well and they did. Not only were the photos good, I have managed to push myself to learn something new. It was out of my comfort zone but it was worth it.

While I was taking photos at the event, one of the guests at the gathering turned to me and said "your gift will make a way for you". Even though I thought she said it casually, I didn't take it lightly. When I got home that day, I began to meditate on what she said and I also continued to pray about it.

A while after that woman said that word of prayer; I encountered how gifts can truly make a way for someone. I experienced it through our son. I shared in Chapter 6 that he was given an almost new guitar because someone noticed he could play well. This goes to show that your gifts can showcase you. They can make a way for you even where you least expect. Although we had planned to buy a guitar but we didn't need to anymore because our son's gift showcased him and earned him a new guitar.

When I looked back, I can also see that my gifts have made many ways for me. It has actually been making ways for me from back in the day, only I didn't pay attention until the prayer that women said opened my eyes to what my gifts had done for me in the past too. Just by using my gifts of writing in the university, I got accommodation on campus throughout my stay in the university aside from the year I put in my application late. I also made money from selling and styling clothes in the university. Presently in my life, my gift has propelled my life forward in many ways I could never imagine. All praises be to God.

Your gifts will make a way for you if you truly take the time to discover them, embrace them and own them. What you have inside of you can help you better your life and help you fulfill specific purpose for your life. Your gift can turn from just a potential locked away inside of you to fulfill real purpose for your life and the life of other people too.

This is another reminder not to waste your gift because it will make a way for you. It may not be immediately when you start using it but at some stage and it will be worth it.

Now, time to grab your notebook! Do this simple exercise:

- What is one thing you have always been afraid to do or learn? You do every other thing but you leave this one thing out; what is that thing?
- Write an action point on how to achieve that thing.

Well done, you are doing great.

CHAPTER 11

YOU MUST BE WILLING TO SERVE

I mentioned in Chapter 6 that I head a group where I share beauty, fashion tips, and motivation to inspire different women from different parts of the world. I basically look for information to share with the group at least 4-5 times a week.

Doing that takes time, it takes effort but it is worth it knowing that I am meeting the need of others by sharing things they may not know or may struggle to find themselves.

Before I went ahead to create the Power Dressers group, I was writing for two other groups. While doing that, it looked as though I was servicing other people's vision but really, I was preparing and polishing my crafts for my own future. When I eventually started my own group, I had mastered the act of managing a group.

I also talked about my experience being an impromptu photographer, that bold step ignited some photography skills in me and the prayer that the woman said changed my orientation and perceptions about my gifts and how gifts can truly make a way for one.

Sometimes, you have to humble yourself enough to serve other people so you can learn from them. When you serve other people and serve diligently, doors of knowledge will open to you. You will learn new skills that money can't buy.

Serve if you need to. It will never go to waste. Trust me, you will learn at least one thing. That one thing will come in handy someday. That day could be the day when God will showcase you and what you can offer. Sometimes you may need to work for free. Do it diligently and whole- heartedly and when you start working on your own, you will find out that you will do your own job diligently too.

More about working for free or willingness to serve, when I talked about self-development earlier in chapter 5, I talked about the skills my husband acquired. These skills helped him to be where he is now. At one point, when he went back to the University, he had to do some work placement. The only position he got was an unpaid one. We asked ourselves what were we going to do? As a father who is passionate about providing for his family, how were we going to cope? I encouraged him to go on and that we will be fine. On my income and our savings, we were fine. The skills he acquired on that work placement positioned him where he is today. Not a lot of people have the skills he has and this is an advantage to him in his current role doing what he loves. In summary, you must be willing to serve even if you do not get paid. It will never be a waste.

If while serving other people you waste time, resources, or lacking in zeal, you will do the same when you eventually start working by yourself or for yourself. Ecclesiastes 9 vs 10 says: "Whatsoever thy hand findeth to do, do it with thy might; for there is no work, nor device, nor knowledge, nor wisdom, in the grave, whither thou goest".

Do whatever you do diligently and with all of your might. You will be surprised how God rewards you and takes you from where you are to where you desire to be. If you are faithful when God gives you little, He will be glad to give you so much more. Make yourself worthy of more.

Don't forget, whatever your hands find to do, do it well.

Now do this simple exercise in your gift book:

- What is one thing you are doing voluntarily right now? Remind yourself to do it diligently and with all of your might.

Well done, you are doing super great.

CHAPTER 12

DON'T LET YOUR GIFT BE ABUSED FROM SERVICE

When you start using your gifts, you may not know as much as the people who have made success from using their gifts. And that was why I suggested in Chapter 4 to get a Mentor who shares the same vision as you. From my experience, a mentor will know about things that will prevent you from using your gift carelessly or in a way that people will abuse your gifts. Learn from their experience and avoid common mistakes by having a mentor.

A lot of people love people who will help them for free. People love people who will do things for them without paying anything for the service. There is nothing wrong with that because it is always a good idea to give when we need to. Be mindful though of giving too much attention to time wasters and users who will take advantage of you when you serve them.

There is also a group of people with a sense of entitlement; they are the ones who feel like it is their right for you to do things for them whenever they want you to. Beware of this and be careful about it. While it is important to give, it is more important to be fulfilled while giving. In fulfillment, you can find rewards and be blessed. What is the point in giving when you give grudgingly?

One of the reasons why your gifts have been given to you is to help others. Your gift is not your own alone to use and enjoy. You must be ready to share, bless and serve others with your gifts. Let me show you what I mean:

"We have different gifts; according to the grace given to us. If a man's gift is prophesying, let him use it in proportion to his faith. If it serving, let him serve; if it is teaching, let him teach; if it is encouraging, let him encourage; if it is contributing to the needs of others, let him give generously; if it is leadership, let him govern diligently; if it is showing mercy, let him do it cheerfully." (Romans 12:6-8)

From that reading, you will notice that although this gift may have been given to you, the instruction is for you to use it to serve and help others. For example, one says, if it is teaching, "let him teach"; this means you should not keep your gift of teaching to yourself but to help others. This is a commandment that has to be obeyed. So although this is your gift, you must give room for others to benefit from it.

Aside from my love for fashion, beauty and writing, I have also been given the gift of encouragement. And because I am commanded to use my gift to help others, I use my gift of encouragement every time I have the opportunity to do so. Every time I speak or write the words of encouragement, I do so boldly and a lot of times I surprise myself. Your gifts come with boldness and you do it so uniquely, so don't waste it.

With my gift of encouragement, I have been able to encourage many to develop their gifts and start pursuing what they love to do; I have in so many times spoken comforting words to people when they are in trouble and my gift of encouragement is one of the reasons why this book had to be written. Even though, I am still on a journey of ensuring that all my own potentials become fulfilled purpose, I am determined to bring as many people along with me by using my gift of encouragement to serve.

Another way I use my gift in service is that I write helpful contents on the blog to a wide range of audience. And because it is free, a lot of people go there, read and benefit from what I share. Through this, I have had so many offers of paid opportunities given to me.

To be able to gain, you must be able to give. You give, you serve, and then you gain. With your gift you can help others and in the place of service you get rewarded. Have the mindset of helping others and in doing so, many opportunities will come knocking. A lot of successful business people use this simple approach of giving and getting back and it works all the time. So far, it has worked for me. Give, you will get back. Be patient so you can see it happen.

Finally on serving and giving, always remember that it is not always about the money. Money is good but it will come through genuine willingness to serve and help others. Jim Rohn says, "it is not always about the money but the journey". Let your focus be the journey and not the money.

BE READY TO GET PAID

When serving and helping others is your motivation, paid opportunities will come. While it is important to serve and give, it is also very important to be ready to get paid. What I mean is that you should know what to charge when the paid opportunities come so you do not work for less than you are worth.

It is best to know from the start or at an early stage when you start using your gifts if you will be seen as a "business" or a hobby. If your intention is to make money out of your gift or what you have, it is best for you to package yourself well and present yourself to the outside world that you mean business.

It is okay not to know if you want to turn your passion into business initially, I felt that way too when I first started using my gifts. With time, I felt the urge to start treating my gift like a "brand". In simple words, I felt the urge to take my gift from potential of making money to actually making money. The urge will come; you will feel it because the more time you invest in yourself and in what you do, the more of it you would want. Wanting more does not mean you are greedy, it means you are ready to take your potential into real purpose.

In reality, when you treat your gift like a hobby or leisure, people will also see it that way. If you nurture your gift or treat it like it is precious to you, people will see it that way too and they will help you treat it that way.

Now do this simple exercise. Write down in your "gift book":

- What is one potential of making money you have but have not actually thought about monetizing?
- What is the next step you can take to monetize it?

Well done.

CHAPTER 13

HERE IS THE PURPOSE & NOT JUST A POTENTIAL

What is a Potential?

Potential simply means latent qualities or abilities that may be developed and lead to future success or usefulness. You can also refer to potential as something that is inherent in a person; it is something that is within you or inborn. In very simple terms, potential can be referred to as something you can do effortlessly.

Purpose on the other hand is to achieve a proposed thing for a specific reason. It can also mean a reason for which something is done. For example, the purpose of writing this book is to encourage people to use their gifts to fulfil specific purpose for their lives.

When you start using your gifts, you will feel a sense of fulfillment each time you do something towards the goal you want to achieve. I feel a sense of fulfillment each time I do something towards achieving a specific goal I have set for myself. For example, each chapter I write of this book brings me a sense of fulfillment and joy. The fulfillment comes because I am taking the potential of being an Author toward the purpose of being a published Author. I smile at the fact that after this book is finished and published I can simply say to anyone that I am not only a writer but also a published author of a book. Isn't that awesome?

That feeling is not too different from finishing from a med school when you can boldly or confidently say to people that you are no more a med student but you are a Doctor. In this case, you would have taken the possibility or potential of being a Doctor into a purpose of being a Doctor.

Whatever your gift is, your goal should be to take it from just a latent potential to turning it into a purpose. If you can do something effortlessly but you don't do anything about it, although you can do that thing, it will remain a potential forever until you do something about it.

If your gift is singing for example, continue to practice and build on your gift but let your aim be to create great music that can impact people whenever they hear you sing. When you do this, you take your potential of blessing or impacting others into the purpose of blessing or impacting them with your music.

If your gift is drawing, photography, writing, teaching, encouraging, or whatever it is, your aim must be to always use that gift to reach as many people as possible. If you can monetize your gifts, it will be a purpose fulfilled for you as well.

GIVE YOURSELF A PAT ON THE BACK

When we fail at anything, we get angry or we blame ourselves for the mistakes we may have made. While that is okay, it is important not to linger on for too long on the mistakes you may have made. Instead focus on the things you have done right and encourage yourself that next time will be better. So don't linger on too long on mistakes of your past. Prepare your mind to try again so you can do well. You never want to go into a new thing feeling defeated already. Start fresh and believe you will succeed.

Achieving anything takes time, preparation, practice, and effort. Even when we try our best not to, it is part of life to make mistakes and there is nothing wrong with it. What that goes to show is that you are trying at something. The people who don't try, play it safe. They do not have the possibility of making mistakes. They are in their comfort zone. Because you are trying outside of your comfort zone, when you do achieve anything, you should be rewarded!

I used to be very hard on myself if I did anything wrong. A friend of mine changed my perception about beating myself up when I fail. Since then, my orientation changed from beating myself up to encouraging myself to try again. It is also scriptural that when you fall, you should rise again according to Proverbs 24 vs. 16. Each time I fail at anything, I do my best to try again till I get the result I desire.

When you do well or when you a take a step towards achieving your set goal, remember to reward yourself. Reward yourself with what you think you are worth or what you think you deserve. In my case, sometimes I take myself out to get some coffee in any café I fancy and sometimes, I get myself some lingerie. Rewarding yourself motivates you to do more because then you are looking forward to getting more rewards. I am looking forward to treating myself when I finish writing this book.

Now do this simple exercise in your notebook:

- What is one particular thing you have failed at?
- Is there an action plan you want to take to retry that thing to achieve success? If so, take action. If not, let it go.
- When you achieve that goal, what reward will you like to give to yourself? Now, write that down too and let it be your push to achieve that goal.

Well done, you are doing great.

CHAPTER 14

YOU NEED A PLAN

It is very important to know if your hobby will be your business or not. It is okay not to know at first because eventually you will figure out what to do. But to be able to succeed at anything, you have to set goals. You need to set some immediate goals, short-term goals, and some long-term goals.

IMMEDIATE GOALS

Your immediate goals are the things you want to achieve quickly or as soon as you start using your gifts. They are goals you want to achieve now, today or immediately. An example of this could be for you to apply to get a placement for an internship or training to develop your gift.

SHORT-TERM GOALS

Your short-term goals are your confidence builder. They are the ones that will lead into your long-term goals. Your short-term goals are the things you want to achieve in the near future. For example within 6 months to 2 years after you start using your gift.

For example, a short-term goal I set for myself is to finish writing this book within 3-6 months. To achieve that goal, no matter what I was doing, I committed to writing a portion of this book daily. I set a timer for a minimum of 2 hours a day with 15 minutes break within the 2-hour period.

Another short-term goal I set for myself within another 3 month period was to finish editing, publishing, and launching live and online. Because my set goals are realistic, this motivated me to work within my time frame so I could achieve the goal. I have to say that setting realistic goals does not make you a lazy person; it makes you work at your pace with low level of stress or tension, which in my experience leads to being more productive.

LONG-TERM GOALS

Your long-term goals are the things you dream about; they are your future. They are the ones you want to achieve in say 2 to 5 years or 5 to10 years after you start using your gifts. Although business these days is changing; it is good to have long-term goals to give you an overall vision but be flexible to adapt to change along the way. You need a combination of immediate, short-term, and long-term goals to keep you in action but also always have a bigger vision in mind.

There is this wise saying that says, "If your dreams don't scare you, they are not big enough". I say it is okay to dream big but don't get lost in your big dreams. Instead pay attention to now and grow into that big dream you've always had.

In your long-term goals, you must prayerfully know where you want your gift to take you. You must know if you want to earn a sustainable income from it. You must also know where you want to be in the future by using your gifts. And finally, you must know if this is something you want to do for the rest of your life or only for a season.

To achieve set goals, they must be realistic and you must have a structure to follow. If you do not have a structure or strategy, it is possible that you keep running around in circles without achieving anything. So be sure to have a structure and a plan that is realistic.

To be able to achieve long-term goals, you may not be able to do it on your own; you may need help from people who work and are professionals in that field. One way to do this is by working with a business strategist or life coach. Sometimes when people hear business strategists or life coaches, thinking this service is not affordable scares them. Consider though that getting direction from the beginning can save time and money. I encourage you to always ask and consider how you can learn from others' experiences and specialty.

WRITE THEM DOWN

Writing things down is the best way to keep track of what you want to do, how you want to do it, where you are, and where you want to be.

The process is known as journaling. Journaling is different from writing in your dairy. You can write in your dairy anywhere. Journaling is different because you can focus on specific things like prayers, goals, accomplishments, etc.

Cultivate the habit of writing things down so you can keep track of everything but most importantly, let that be a reminder for you to achieve your goals. I mentioned in the introduction of this book that when I got the inspiration to write this book, I was in the kitchen. I immediately left what I was doing to write down what God was laying in my heart at that particular point in time. If I didn't obey then, I may not be writing this book.

As I continued to write this book, I have the book journal beside me. As I write, I get ideas on what to write next, I purse, write it down so I do not forget and continue to do my writing. I also carry that book with me all the time in case I get inspiration on what to write when I am out and about.

That process of pursing to write things that click with me helps me to do more and to be productive. Research shows that when you write things down, you are not likely to forget and you are likely to follow through on doing that particular thing. When you just keep thinking about the thing in your head, on the other hand, you are less likely to remember and to follow through. Cultivate the habit of writing things down. You will make things much easier on yourself and have to rely less on remembering everything you think of to contribute to your goals and projects.

I read about Octavia Butler a while ago and how she used journaling to write and program her life the way she wanted it to be. One of the things Octavia Butler did was that she journaled her prayers and began to call the things that were not yet reality as though they already were. That is scriptural. I also mentioned that you have to have some faith in order to reach your goals. That is also scriptural (Romans 4:17b)

When you write your goals, and believe in them, that is when you believe that you can achieve them; this is called faith. For things you cannot see, you must believe them to come while you are working at them. (James 2:14 -26)

Since I read about Octavia, I would write the things I wanted down and believe them as I continued to work at them. I remembered writing down that I wanted to be featured on the cover of a magazine. Initially I was featured on the Guardian, that wasn't what I prayed or hoped for. Even though that was good, I wrote down again that I wanted to be on the cover of a magazine. The opportunity eventually came and I made it to the cover of a magazine.

When the magazine invited me to be on their cover, in their letter, they said, "there are a lot of Content creators / Bloggers we want to feature from all around the world but we want you to be on the cover". I was specific in asking, I believed it, kept doing my work, and I achieved it.

You may be wondering what being on the cover of a magazine did for me. It opened the door for a lot of people who didn't know me to get to know what I do and how they could work with me. This was a wonderful moment for me and helped me believe for bigger things to come.

To be a success at using your gifts, it is important to write things down and to believe them. Faith is like a muscle and as you use it and complete your goals, you get stronger and stronger.

Now do this simple exercise in your "gift book":

- Do you have a journal where you write down your thoughts, prayers, goals, and achievements? If you don't, make a note in your "gift book" that you need to get yourself a journal and then set a day to go and get one.
- If you do have a journal for recording your prayers, goals, and achievements, well done to you! Continue to use it and I challenge you to get even more specific in your goals and practice saying those things aloud as though they are already true as you continue pursuing them.

You are doing great!

CHAPTER 15

TIME IS MONEY, DON'T WASTE IT

Everything good takes time to achieve. For you to be able to achieve the goals you have written down, you need time. Time waits for no one, time runs so fast and you cannot afford to waste it. You have to keep moving, as time is moving. Time is one of the most valuable commodities that you have; it is more valuable than money. You can make more money back but you can never make more time back.

Here's what the Bible says about knowing what to do and at what time according to Ephesians 5:16; Pay careful attention, then, to how you walk, not as unwise but as wise, redeeming the time, because the days are evil. Therefore do not be foolish, but understand what the Lord's will is.

Every day you open your eyes; God gives you the gift of today. Before you woke up, that day wasn't guaranteed just like tomorrow is not guaranteed either. Now that you have that day, it is important to take charge of the day by living intentionally, positive, hopeful, pursuing your goals, and being a blessing to others. On the other hand, if you are not careful, you could live unintentionally, negative, discouraged, worrying and being enemies with everybody. You can see the former is more profitable or rewarding and the latter, a waste of time, and the gift of today you were given.

For each and every day you live to witness, take charge of it, invest it, utilize it and maximize it to the fullest. You do not have the time to involve yourself in things that do not concern you; you just do not have the time. Instead focus on how to use the 86,400 seconds or 24 hours you have been given on the day. You have the same 24 hours as any other person even with the richest people in the world. What you do with your time is what is most important and what will determine your outcome in life. Would you rather use your time wisely or foolishly?

If there are things coming your way that you cannot sacrifice your time to do, it is important to say NO to them. For example, No, I am not going to watch television when I am supposed to be studying or I am not going to go to the shopping mall when I am supposed to be writing my school project or I am not going to go to the cinema when I am supposed to be spending time with my sick mother etc.

One importance of planning ahead and taking charge of your time I have learnt is that you can actually set realistic goals and work as planned to achieve them. Setting goals should be a daily ritual for you so you can achieve what you want to achieve.

If you are one who goes with the flow, leaves things unplanned, fights unnecessary battles, or just handles things as they come up; you probably won't achieve many big goals. This is because those other things that are not important will keep taking your time. It is also possible that when you are now ready to take on working on your goal, you may be too tired to work on them and then your 24hours is gone and you can't account for what you did with it. Your only option is now to wait for the next day, which is not guaranteed.

Not planning your time according to your priorities and allowing things to just move you from this to that will not allow you move forward in your purpose. You don't have to be planned minute by minute but you do need to prayerfully consider how you should invest each day.

When you don't create a routine or allocate time to everything that has to be done, you could have a lot of time at hand and still not be doing anything. You will just realize that in 24 hours, you can't really account for what you did. If you are not careful, this circle of not knowing what you do with your time could keep repeating itself until you take charge of your time.

To take charge of your time, you can:

1. Plan or map out your day everyday

This simply means, put down time for everything you have to do on daily basis. Be specific in allocating time to what you want to do. For example you can put down from;

9am-10am: an hour of study to learn how to start a blog or how to learn graphics design.

Say something like; to start at 9am, take a break at 9.20am and return at 9.30am to continue.

You can also give yourself a break of another 20 minutes before going into your next task. What I mean is if you finish studying at 10am; give yourself till 10.20am before you go on to the next task. Continue your day like that so you are not rushed and can still achieve your goals for the day.

2. Set realistic goals and write down steps to achieve them.

For example today, I want to research where to develop my gift of singing. In this case you want to write down; contact details of where the training is done; when to ring them, when to visit them to see if they can help etc.

It is not enough to just write what to do down; the most important thing is to establish how you will do them and that is how you can achieve them.

3. Don't over load your day with what to do or too much.

It can be overwhelming. Let your goals be realistic always. Always remember that setting realistic goals does not mean you are lazy. Rather, it will help you work at your own pace and without stress, which leads to being productive.

4. Don't go where you have not planned to go and don't do what you have not planned to do.

That random phone call doesn't have to change your plan for day. If you have not planned it before, don't consider taking it on board.

Once you take charge of your time, you won't just go with the flow. When you don't take charge of your time by planning, you just go with the flow. Going with the flow in most cases, will make it very difficult for you to achieve anything. When you set goals, and then make a plan for achieving them, you can do so much more.

For example, if anyone asks you for a favour and their request is for you to help them coordinate an event in your local community center, you can respond to them by saying, "thank you so much for the opportunity. Can I check my schedule and get back to you in 2 days?"

Once you respond to them like that, you have bought time to think about your availability and to ensure that your routine can permit you to do all that is required of you. Once you check your to do list within the 2 days, you can then go back to them with your answer which could either be a, "Yes I would have the time to help." or a "No, I will not be able to help." This way, when you commit to do something, you can be sure to do it well.

You must be able to tell if you can spare the time to do other things than what you are already doing and consider whether this request is important or immediate related to the other goals you have set for yourself. If you set goals and work your plan, you will quickly be able to tell if the thing that has been asked of you is a distraction to your set goals.

For example, recently, I was invited to anchor a Programme. When I got the email from the host, I read and acknowledged it by replying. I made sure to let the host know that I am grateful for the opportunity but the time they wanted me to anchor the Programme was not good for me. I didn't have to tell them the reason; I just said the time wasn't good for me because I was working on other things. At the time, I was working on this book because I had a timeline to finish it; if I took on something else, my plans will be disrupted and I may struggle to find time to meet up with my set plan. They then said, give us the time that works for you and I did. I did the anchoring and I did it well and in my time too.

The opportunity I was offered to anchor that Programme was important but not urgent. However, this book is important and urgent. You see the difference? If something is important but not urgent, it can wait. On the other hand, if something is important and urgent, it shouldn't wait. This book to me is very important and urgent because I have a time line to finish it. If something is important to you and urgent, attend to it immediately till you get results. As for things that are important but not urgent, let them wait till you finish the urgent and important ones.

A lot of us feel guilty for saying NO or saying our terms, please don't. It is important to be certain you will be able to do things for people or help them. If you can't, let them know. Although you may not be able to help, this does not mean you do not care about them, you do but you just can't make the time then. Even though you can't help, show compassion by asking if they have been able to sort out what they needed help for.

You do not need to apologise for taking charge of your time. Your time is yours to use, use it wisely. Having said that, if time permits you to help others, please do, it is a labour of love and God will reward you for offering it.

Tunji Babatunde, a Preacher, Motivational speaker and a Life Coach once said, "if you don't have work to do, people will give you work to do". This statement is true because it is when you are not busy enough that people assume you have the time to help them do things while they are gone to do their own job or to do their own business or are working towards achieving their own goals.

People who reach out to others for random help always are not goal setters themselves. Goal setters always have at the back of their minds that other people may have plans or projects they are doing too. There may be emergencies, which could warrant you to reach out to people urgently but people who reach out to others randomly for help are not normally organised. If you want people to help you do things, give them enough time or notice and vice versa. Plan your time and be organized, it is the key to achieving purposeful goals.

If you are working on a project or developing your gift, it is important to make that project your priority so you can achieve the goal you want. Taking on other unimportant things when your focus should be to finish your project is not a wise move because you may never achieve your goal. Instead you will be surrounded by lots of unfinished projects, which could be very discouraging

.

CHAPTER 16

GET PAID, YOU DON'T WORK FOR FREE

Now, you have been working on yourself for some time. You have invested time, money, and effort in developing your gifts. It is also possible that by now you have mastered your crafts like a pro. It is also okay if you still feel like you are not a pro yet. If you don't feel like a pro yet, don't stop working on yourself and developing your gift.

SHOULD I WAIT

I know you may be wondering if you should wait till you are a "pro" at what you do before you start making money.

My simple answer is NO. Why? Don't forget you have invested time and money on yourself to develop your gift. You have denied yourself of some of the things you like or love doing etc. Yes, the ideal thing is to help people with your gifts but you cannot continue to give your services away for free.

Remember that saying that people do not appreciate what they haven't paid for. To some extent, I tend to believe that. Look at our everyday lives, when people give us gifts we do not like, we just dump the "thing" somewhere and we won't be bothered about it. However when people give us good gifts, we tend to keep the "thing" safely and look forward to using it.

When you use your gift on people carelessly, you are not doing yourself any good. Below are examples of some of the things that may happen to you:

1. You may be taken advantage of.
2. You may not be able to invest in and improve yourself further.
3. You may just be wasting your time and gift.
4. You may end up being tired, weary, and then give up.

You can use your gift to support non-profit or charities or start one yourself. However, if you use your gift to help people who can pay for your service, you should charge them for the service you have rendered. In some cases, charities and non-profits have a budget to pay for services, if this is the case, get paid except of course you want to support them by spending your time to help them. I do this all the time when I get invited to speak for charities; I do not charge them for that.

In Chapter one, I mentioned the friend who did my CV for £150.00, even though she could have done it for free as a friend, she charged me for it because she used her skill set and time and she got paid for it. Do I think she deserved to get paid? Yes I do because she has used her gift, time, and energy. I also said it was not until after she did my CV that I got a job offer. So it was worth it because she knew something I didn't know and that did the magic for me.

Also look at it this way; when people go to work, they get paid whether weekly, biweekly, or monthly. They do not work for free. They do the job and they get paid for it. Even though it is your gift or talent, you should get paid or rewarded for serving or working.

One entrepreneur mindset to have is to always get rewarded or paid for rendering a service. I have learnt to pay people when they offer their services to me so they too can have money in their purses. I pay them what they are worth. Ensure to always charge what your service is worth. Enter some terms of payment or agreement with your clients or customers before you go on with their work. If your agreement reads for them to finish payment before you deliver, ensure they stick to it and on your own path, deliver what you promised them.

When I started doing freelance writing via my blog, I didn't charge anything for it; that was deliberate. At the time when I didn't charge for all the services I rendered, I was mastering the art of creative writing and I gave myself about 6months to 9months to master the art of writing. While writing isn't an exact science, you can develop and broaden on how wide your imagination can take you by writing more. The more writing I did, the better I became at it. Look at me now, I am writing a book!

By the way, creating content or writing takes time. Sometimes on a Sunday, I sit for up to 4 hours with little breaks here and there to create just one blog for clients and for free too. That is the price I had to pay and I took it very seriously because I was hopeful for results that one day, I would get paid for all the sacrifices I have been making. Another mindset of an entrepreneur is to be willing to put in the work and make sacrifices.

After a while, a lot of people started commending my writing. It was then I knew that I was good to start charging for writing. When I became sure that my skills were enough to make money, I researched what Freelance Writers charged and I compared that to what I could offer and began to charge for writing.

For all the other blogs I was servicing for free, I began to drop them one at a time by letting them know that I now charge for that service. A lot of them didn't believe it when I announced to them that I now charge for the service of writing. I made sure to let them know that writing takes time and a lot of effort, so I do not do it for free anymore. I did that because they make money from there business because of the content I create for them. Out of all those blogs, I only retained two who were willing to pay for the service I rendered and I made sure I served them well. It didn't matter that the other ones let go because I wasn't being paid anyway; it goes to show that they were taking advantage of my time, gifts, and skills.

Even though I consider creative styling a gift and I am passionate about it, gifts are not enough, I invested money in learning image consulting. Because I have studied to show myself approved, I also stopped styling for free. I invested money being trained as an Image Consultant so to get rewarded for my self-development; I started charging for that as well. You see; I have been able to monetize my gifts.

When people make money and can afford to pay for the service you offer them, charge them and let them pay you what you are worth. You should also know that it is not your place to assume people can't afford to pay you. Charge them what your time is worth and let them decide if they can afford it.

BE FLEXIBLE IN CHARGES

One business point I learnt from my husband is to be open in charging for the services you render. This is one of the advantages of working for yourself. It is also important to assess your location and the people you serve to determine how much to charge. Of course what you are worth matters but what is the point in charging what the people you serve can't pay?

When you are open in charging for your service, you won't close the door of service on the people who truly and genuinely can't pay. What this means is for example, if you charge £40.00 for a service and a client can only afford to pay £30.00, do your best to inform them what you can offer them at that price and serve them well like you would serve the client who paid £40.00. That is honesty and it will open more doors of opportunities to you. Don't say because they paid less you would serve them less, you will be doing damage to your reputation.

This open charge approach may not work for everyone but so far it has worked for me. It also goes to show you are compassionate and you care about the people you serve. Also, it shows you are passionate about what you do and your willingness to help others.

When it comes to offering a service as an entrepreneur, don't give your service away for free. In fact, never work for free. The only time you should give your service away for free is if you choose to use your gift as a means of giving, marking a special occasion, or helping a charity you believe in.

YOU ARE NOT CHEAP, YOU ARE SMART

I mentioned above that it is okay to be open in charges. While that is okay, it is also very important not to put yourself in a position where people will take advantage of you because they know already that you love to help. What I mean is this; even though you are open in charges, have a minimum amount you can charge for a particular service and that should be the least you can charge for that service. If you like call it your "minimum pay". Just like there is a cut of minimum wage if you work in an organization. In this case, you don't get minimum wage but you can create a minimum pay for your skill.

Aim to earn really high but remember you are not cheap for reducing your price but you are smart. I have heard the saying "high-end clients". I love that term but to be a strong and continuous earner, I believe in having the flexibility in pricing because if you are not flexible in pricing, you may be losing money.

Take for example, two supermarkets: Tesco and Aldi. If I walk into Tesco and the price is too high, I will walk right straight to Aldi to buy similar for the price I can afford. Does that mean what I bought in Aldi for cheaper is bad? No it isn't. Aldi is just being smart by making their prices affordable for the same product. If you compare the quality of what you bought in Tesco with that of Aldi, you will find out that you have bought the same thing in different packaging.

While it is best to target high-end clients who can pay big money, it is also good to be able to serve everyday people who do not have the luxury of paying so much. While it is good to consider being flexible or open in pricing; bear in mind, to always have a minimum charge so the time you spend in serving them is proportionate to the money you are paid.

It is okay for your goal to be to serve high-end clients, you may not be able to make any money if there are other people who do exactly the same thing you do for less and would add the same value. Remember the Tesco and Aldi illustration above?

Instead of not making money at all because your target is only to serve high-end clients, why not use the strategy of "price matching". What I mean is this: if the people who do the same thing as you charge XYO, why not charge XYO to be able to match their price and continue to make money while using your gifts. When you gain momentum, enough experience and you create a reputable and solid brand, you won't have to reduce your price any more. Until then, be flexible in charges and you will always make money.

Remember, you are not cheap for charging less; you are smart because you will always make money.

Grab your notebook and do this simple exercise:

- Do you know how much you should be charging for your service? If you don't know, research how much people earn for doing the same thing as you. Good news is everything is online. For example, you can simply Google; how much does a Personal Shopper earn hourly. Now you get the idea.

You are well on your way now! You are doing great.

HAVE AN ENTERPRENUER MINDSET

Now that you are making money, you can consider yourself an Entrepreneur. Your gift is no more a hobby but a business because you now make money. You have graduated from just a potential to fulfilling purpose. Wow, well done, you've come a long way.

As an Entrepreneur, your aim should always be to gain hundred percent profits. There is profit and there is loss. Ensure to minimize your losses at all times.

Let's see some factors an entrepreneur must consider always:

1. Have a Brand name and a Brand message

Your brand name could be anything you want it to be but have a reason or know your why for it. Your brand name could be as simple as your name. For example, Mojisola Obazuaye. Fashion stylist, Speaker, Writer and Digital Content Creator.

Digital Content Creator covers Mojisola Obazuaye as a Blogger and as a YouTube Creator. It is that simple!

The first and the most important thing to consider is the message of the brand you are trying to create. You have to have a clear message of what you do. For example if what you do is Coaching or Mentoring, state it as it is so people can easily understand it. Your message can simply be helping people (men or women) identify their gifts and develop them from potential to purpose.

2. Decision-making

You must be able to make decisions. Don't sit on the fence about things. You could take your time to respond but be decisive. Know what you want and go for it. For example, while it is okay to be flexible in charges, be sure to stick with what you charge or the minimum pay.

As an entrepreneur, you should have a mindset of creating a fortune. This means you should aim to make more than someone who works for others. Also bear in mind that in business, there could be a fluctuation in the amount you make.

3. Be ready to pay the price and outsource what you hate to do

You have to be willing to do all the work that goes with being a boss or an entrepreneur or a leader. You have to serve, give, make sacrifices, pray, and do everything that goes with being an entrepreneur.

For things you can't do or things you struggle with, outsource them to a professional in that field, so you can have the time to do the things you truly enjoy. When you do this, you put money in other people's pocket and their business grows too. In return, it makes your own life easier and run smoothly.

4. Don't be afraid to fail

Being afraid restricts you from going far. Don't be too cautious about trying or failing. Try and if you fail, you would know you tried. If you ever fail, learn from it and do your best the next time you try again. Always remember failing means you are trying. If you ever fail, try again.

5. Bring Others with You

You have spent a lot of time developing and investing in yourself. Now it is the time to teach others how. An entrepreneur must be willing to show others the way as he or she walks in the way. This is one important life lesson I learnt from my late father.

Being an entrepreneur or a leader now means you have been given the chance to take care of others; it is not just a title or a rank. What this means is that you have been given the chance to serve from the position of a leader. Leaders don't rule from a high horse, they help their followers climb on the horse too. Leaders don't bully, intimidate or demand respect, they earn it through service.

6. Get Clients first

Turning your gift into a real business is not a child's play. It takes a lot of commitment. In my humble opinion, the best way to know if you are in business is when you are serving clients already and making money. Don't spend too much money on websites, marketing materials, etc. and then begin to look for clients. Look for clients first and let the money they pay you take care of all of those other things.

Clients first and then business plan, structure and every other thing follows. Earn while you learn and then add to your business as you can afford to do so.

7. Study

To be a successful entrepreneur, you have to study, study and study more. You have to invest in yourself more and you have to find out how things work. When you find out information about anything, don't leave them in your head, write them down preferably in your journal and let that be a reminder for you to achieve them. You may not be able to do all you find out but you should find out all you can do. John Maxwell says, "Never think that what you can do doesn't matter because it does".

The things you need to study are the things that will change your economic, social, spiritual and personal life. Study success if you wish to be successful. Study happiness if you wish to be happy. Study wealth if you wish to be wealthy etc. Study so you do not leave anything to chance.

8. Save

When you start making money from your gifts or business, it is important to save. Save some of the money you make, invest some of it in profitable things and re-invest some of it in your business so you can grow your business. If you make money and spend lavishly on other things other than your business, it will be hard for you to grow your business. Never spend more than you earn and don't be wasteful.

Money managers or coaches always say, "invest in things that yield more money and from the interest of those investments, you can indulge". What this means is from the profits of your investment, you can buy that new bag you want for example or go on that holiday or visit a spa and on and on.

9. Learn to Rest

All work and no play they say make Jack a dull boy. You work hard; learn to rest your body so you can be well and strong to enjoy all your good works. There is no point working hard, acquiring wealth but too sick to enjoy it. Rest well, feed well and play too. Leaders, entreprenuer and bosses deserve some rest too. I love the way one of my friends puts it, she says, "work hard but play harder".

Amazingly, we learn when playing. We feel refreshed and great ideas come to us when we play. Too much work can really make Jack a dull boy.

One great life lesson amongst other things I learnt and wrote about on www.mojintouch.com was about the recent visit of the owner and founder of Facebook, Mark Zuckerberg's to Africa (Nigeria and other countries) for work. Although it was all about work, he and his team made the time to play. They visited a Safari in

Nairobi, Kenya and they also visited a music studio in Lagos, Nigeria. What this tells me is that; it is important to work hard but it is also important to rest and play. Find a balance so you are not stressed or worked up.

CHAPTER 17

BE AVAILABLE, STOCK YOUR SHOP

To be a success at anything you do, you must always stock your shop. What does this mean? Your shop could be a physical shop if you sell physically, your shop could be online if you sell or offer some sort of service and your shop could be your brain if you are a mentor or a coach or a writer etc. In my own case, my shop or office is my website, YouTube channel, my brain and online presence.

If for any reason you will be gone for a while or you will not be available to do what you do, let the people you serve know you won't be around. Don't give them the chance to go to another. If they wait for you for a while and you are nowhere to be found, they will look for other options. Having said that, some people will stay no matter what. The reason why some people would stay is how you serve. If you serve with all your might, they see that… but when you serve just for the money, they see that too.

If you are gone for too long or you leave your shop without stock, it is an opportunity for your competitors to take your place before you return. Always ensure your shop is stocked and if you are going to be gone for a while, a courtesy call, an email, a text message or a newsletter would be ideal to let them know you won't be around. If possible, make provision for how to take great care of them while you are gone. For example, if I am going to be gone for a while, I write enough blogs that would see me through my absence and set them to self-publish at a particular time and on a particular day. I then follow up on comments and queries anywhere I am in the world. I do the same for my YouTube channel too. A lot of people don't actually get to know I am away because the shop is stocked for them with what they want.

If you have a physical shop, make sure that you stock up on what people buy so when they come around, they can find what they need. Take for example; we have an Aldi beside a Tesco. If I walk into Tesco looking for my favourite brand of milk and they do not have it. The next step would be for me to simply walk into Aldi to see if they have it. If they have it, I buy from there and won't be bothered provided I have what I needed.

If I return to Tesco in 2 days and the same thing happens, I will simply go back to Aldi and see if they have it. If they do; I will buy from them and walk away.

The next time I am out shopping to buy the same milk, I will go directly to Aldi instead of going to Tesco first. In my mind, I would conclude that for the past two visits to Tesco, they do not have the milk; so as not to waste time, I would go straight to Aldi because they will always have it.

Same approach can be used for services, if you leave a void for your customers to go somewhere else, they will go. Don't take chances and never forget that your competitors may be as good as you. Do all you can for your customers to have a reason to stay with you. Let your price be right, let your service be spot on, and let it show that you truly care to serve them. Remember each time you won't be available for any period of time, don't just disappear without letting them know that you have a way to serve them even in your absence.

YOU HAVE NOT BEEN SENT TO THEM

In service, no matter how well you serve or how well you do what you do, there will always be people who will not see what you are worth. They will not acknowledge how good you are or how well you do what you do. The only time such people say something is when you make mistakes, do something wrong or fail.

For such people, you have not been sent to them. They do not know your worth or acknowledge what you do so do not worry about them because you have not been sent to them. Do your best not to chase after people who do not know what you are worth; it means you have not been sent to them.

Don't beg people to love or accept you or what you do. When you do, you belittle your God-given potential and abilities and you begin to doubt. Instead, focus on the people who appreciate and celebrate you.

YOU WERE SENT TO THEM

In the previous paragraph, I talked about people you have to run after before they acknowledge you.

For the people you have been sent to, you will not need to beg them, drag them or convince them, they will acknowledge you, celebrate you, buy from you, pay what your service is worth, praise you, and refer others to you. It is a cycle that can be repeated if truly you serve and deliver your best.

The people who follow the cycle I described above are the ones you have been sent to. In return, be sure to celebrate them, offer them your best, and be kind to them so they will always be around.

You weren't sent to serve everyone and that is OK. Don't be afraid to let go of people who don't care and stay where the love is. People thrive where there is love and where they feel appreciated. Offer that to your customers so they will want to keep coming back to your business.

CHAPTER 18

YOUR ENEMIES CAN LOVE YOU

I said in Chapter 5 that you should never go into anything with a negative mindset. This is also one of the characteristics of an entrepreneur that I mentioned earlier. Sometimes in life, even when you have the mindset of a victor, there are people who just won't like you. No, you haven't done anything to them; they just do not like you. Sometimes it may just be due to the potential they have seen in you or a misconception of how they think you have it all. So, let's talk about how to handle these people so you won't get discouraged or be taken off guard when someone doesn't like you or your services.

It is okay for people to feel different about you. You cannot control, command, or change how people feel or what they think about you. However, you can control how you react or respond to what and how they think about you.

Let me share this simple step to deal with people not liking you with you. "When a man's ways are pleasing to the Lord, he makes even his enemies to be at peace with him." (Proverbs 16:7) All you have to do is 1) be in right standing with God and 2) do not forget to pray for them. You will be surprised that by themselves, they will be at peace with you.

Remember, you are not at war with anyone. You are only doing what you are meant to be doing to better your life and to take your potential to fulfill purpose. Most of the time, they are upset with themselves or about something that has nothing to do with you personally.

Every person has his or her own challenges and insecurities they are dealing with. Commit to praying for those who hurt you and be humble enough to ask God to show you in each instance if you have done anything to harm them in any way. God is faithful to show us when we have sinned against others and He will give you the grace to make it right. He will also give you the grace to handle when you come across those who still won't be a fan of yours. Just keep moving forward looking for those that He sent you to serve.

CHAPTER 19

DOES LOCATION MATTER?

If you are willing and obedient, you shall eat the good of the land (Isaiah 1:19)

The above scripture reminds us that no matter where we are, all we have to do is to be obedient and we will benefit from the goodness of the land.

I have heard a lot of people say that they have to move to the happening country or location before they can begin to use their gifts to fulfill their purpose. To some extent, that is true if that is where God wants you to go. But if God does not want you to move to that particular location, no matter what you do, you may not prosper.

Moving to a country or state where God does not want you to move to is like using someone else's talent. If that is not where you are meant to be, you will struggle. I have also heard of people who move to a country because others are moving there; they have had to return to where they were before because where they moved to was not meant for them.

Before you make a big move, ensure to be led by God. If not, you may be wasting your precious time and money. Instead of moving, start where you are and seek the face of God to know if his desire is for you to move. The most important place to be is right where God wants you to be. Pray and be listening for His direction before making any moves.

Do this simple exercise in your gift notebook:

- In your current location, are you striving or thriving?
- If you are striving instead of thriving, write an action plan to seek the face of God. Ask for him to lead you where you should be.
- If you are thriving where you are, take time to praise God for all He is doing in your life!

WHAT YOU HAVE IS ENOUGH, START WITH IT

A lot of us like to wait for the perfect time to begin to use our gifts even when we know what we are good at already. I hate to be the one to break it to you but *there is no such thing as a perfect time.* You may want to write that down and post it above your desk to be reminded of this. God can give you the grace to redeem time but don't allow that to become your permission to waste time. We are to be wise stewards of the resources God gives us. Choose to be someone who doesn't make a habit of wasting time.

You will never have enough time to do *everything* you want to do. For the things that truly matter to you, like using your gifts, you will have to create time to do them. That was why I mentioned in Chapter 15 that it is important to prioritise and learn to say NO to things that are not as important. You must also have a solid plan and quit going with the flow. When you go with the flow, you will end up nowhere.

If, for example, you work full time but you want more in life than your full-time job, this will take extra effort for a season. You will have to make strategic plans and be intentional on how to create time out of your busy life. Believe that it is worth the effort and begin to use your gifts, develop them, and take them from potential to purpose. You do not have to do everything in a day; the idea is to be intentional about what you want to do and progressively take action to achieve your goals.

For example if you spend 2hours on social media daily, you may want to cut down to say 30minutes daily. Use a timer to control yourself. Once your 30minutes is over, log out of all social media and go to work. Making small changes like these will add up! They require a lot of discipline, commitment to self, and the help of God.

Take that bold step to spend a set amount of time on achieving your goals. You may struggle at first; this is even to be expected. But you will eventually get into a routine that works for you and you will be surprised at what you can do when you follow through.

Every time you achieve a goal, give yourself a pat on the back. Rewarding yourself is a great way to encourage yourself to do more and makes it fun along the way. You may not have a lot of money to spend on rewarding yourself. This is where you can get creative. Make a list of things you enjoy doing but haven't done lately because you are working so diligently toward your goal. Some examples could be: reading a book for pleasure, painting your nails, taking a bubble bath, going for a walk, visiting a museum, or giving yourself extra time to catch up with people through phone calls or social media. Your rewards don't have to be costly. They just need to be something you enjoy that you will look forward to once you've completed a goal.

If you can make time to start and follow through, you will see that things will begin to fall in place. You will begin to research who can help you, how you can get the money you need to start that project, and every other thing will begin to fall in place but, it all starts by taking the time to start where you are and with what you have. What you have is the little time you can carve out for yourself. Until you are willing to start with what you have, you may not be able to achieve anything.

CHAPTER 20

DON'T KEEP QUIET

Opportunities may only come but once, so whatever your gift is, you must be prayerful and watchful to take action when the opportunity is there. When you start earning an income by using your gift, it is very important to spread the word. You can also start spreading the word before you are earning an income so people know about you already. Tell people about what you do so as many people as possible can hear about you and what you do.

FRIENDS & FAMILY

The first people that should help you are your friends and family. Let them know about what you are doing. You can simply say something like; Aunty Irene, for the past 9 months, I have been practising make-up artistry after my training in the make-up school. Now, I am helping people do their make-up, please spread the word.

Once you say it to your favourite Aunty Irene, go ahead and tell every member of your family and tell your friends too. Also tell them to tell their friends. From there, word will begin to spread. When people need a make-up artist, they will contact you.

Don't forget that it is okay to give gifts to your friends and family. But always remember that business succeeds when friends and family pay for services rendered to them. For all your friends and family that can afford to pay for the service you render to them, be sure to let them pay for it.

A good business lesson to learn is that you shouldn't have to work for free. When you make money, you can easily turn your passion into a real business and before you know it, you may not need to continue at your job, if you had one. If your desire is to run your own business full time, you will have the opportunity to do so only if you start charging for the service you offer.

Moving from your day job to using your God-given gift full time is a huge step and a testimony of taking your gift from potential to purpose. No one says it is going to be easy at first, but it is doable if you follow through.

Now grab your "gift book" and do this simple exercise:

- Is it your desire to take your potential to purpose by doing what you love full time?

- If so, write down your action plan for how you intend to do it.
- Make a commitment to devote fervent prayer time to this too.

Well done, you are doing great.

WORD OF MOUTH

One of the lessons I learnt from working with the beauty brand I talked about in Chapter 2 is that you should always share the opportunity with people everywhere you go.

When you meet people, always tell them about what you do and how you can be of help to them. Never stop talking to people about what you do, you never can tell when they will need your service. Talking to people about your gifts simply means you are serious and confident about what you do and that you want to go somewhere from doing it. Spreading the word is a way to go get new opportunities and recommendations.

BE SOCIAL

We are in a social era where everything and everyone is online. If you have access to the Internet, use the power of social media to spread the word about what you do. The 3 most popular ones are Twitter, Facebook and Instagram. There are more but those three will do for a start if you are not a social butterfly. Get an account set up on all those platforms and begin to connect with people.

Once you start connecting with people, don't forget to continue to talk about what you do.

ACTIONS SPEAK LOUDER THAN WORDS

For the people you have helped or worked with in the past, try and get testimonials from them. It will be handy to share with your new clients, customers, and every other person that may need your help in the future.

If your work involves taking photos, take good photos, and keep them for your record. They will be handy to show to other people as an example of your work. Allow me share my little photo tricks with you. One of the ways I get people to know about what I do is that I take good photos. I work with a professional photographer who helps me take quality photos. I share all of those photos on all my social network channels and people respond to them out of curiosity. Some of these people like the photos, some click on links included, and the ones who need my service through the photos are convinced that I can help them.

Now remember, taking those photos is not enough; sharing them is the most important thing! Share them on all your social networks and don't forget to continue to talk about what you do. Testimonials are good advertisements on their own, so, ensure to always get them from people you work with. They could end up being more valuable than the profit you made on the initial job you did in the long run. Don't miss out on this way of maximizing your work.

BUSINESS CARDS

I know you may be wondering why you would need business cards. You need them for when you go to events, social gatherings, and any other occasion where you meet up with people and could meet new prospects for your business.

When you speak to people about what you do even if you have a clear message of what you do; they may not be able to take in everything the first time you speak to them. If you hand them your business card, it will be easier for them to remember you and then reach out to you when they need you.

Now do this simple exercise:

- Do you have social media accounts? Now is the time to open them for yourself. Like I suggested the popular ones are Facebook, Instagram, and Twitter.
- Decide on what name you want to be known as and open your account with that name. Once you do, don't forget to keep talking about what you do so as many people as possible can connect with you and reach out to you when they need you.

CHAPTER 21

IT WON'T ALWAYS BE ROSY

In life, there will always be ups and downs or challenges; this is inevitable. I was lucky enough to have a mother that taught me this. She didn't teach me that to scare me but to prepare me for life and the ups and downs that come with it.

As much as there may be challenges, the assurance you have is that in His kindness, God called you to share in his eternal glory by means of Christ Jesus. So after you have suffered a little while, he will restore, support, and strengthen you. He will place you on a firm foundation (1 Peter 5:10). This is an awesome promise that even when trouble or problems or challenges come, you will eventually have victory. So do not worry and do not be afraid. Things have a way of working out when we look up to God.

It is what you do when you are in times of trouble that matters. When there are challenges, take your eyes off those challenges and be thankful for what you have. When you are thankful for what you have, strength comes from dealing with what trouble or problems you may have at hand.

Even though things may not be as rosy as you want them to be, be rest assured that all will eventually be well and more importantly, through you, God will be glorified. If you ever go through anything that may be unpleasant or a trial, God is using such trials to prepare your for victory, good success and outstanding testimonies. Whatever it is you may go through, God will be on time for you. Call on him and He will answer you.

CHAPTER 22

CHARACTER BUILDING

Being in the "public eye" for someone like me was daunting at first because there was criticism from all around. However, I have managed to stay out of trouble online. My line of business; vlogging, blogging, styling and writing requires me to be online and on social media a lot. I had to learn quickly how to deal with the negative aspects of being out there for others to criticize.

Yes, I use social media to promote all of my work but that is not my life. I do have a life outside of social media; my life and the quality time I spend with my beautiful family and my real-life friends.

How have I managed to build the kind of character I am talking about? Being grounded by what I was taught growing up and knowing my worth apart from what others say about me helped build my character and made me strong enough to handle criticism and whatever comes my way. Here are some of the things that have helped shape me and build my character:

TRUST & TRANSPARENCY

When you start making money and people hand their money over to you, ensure you are accountable to the last penny. What that means is to ensure to have how you spend their money documented. In simple terms keep records. Making money is good and allows you to buy the things you need, improve your standard of living, invest in yourself, pay your bills easily, go on holidays and much more. Treat it with respect and handle it well so that you can be trusted with more of it.

Also, it is important for your yes to be yes and your NO to be NO. When you say things, keep to your promise; let your word be your bond. For example, if you tell people that their job will finish in two days. Ensure you finish in two days and let them know you have finished. Bring the end results to them within your specified period. This is one way of building trust, not only for their sake but for yours as well. Each time you fulfill a promise or commitment, you are assuring yourself that you can be trusted to get the job done.

One of the things that have helped me a lot is delivering before time. In this case when I say I will be through in two days, I ensure to finish in one day and make delivery. It makes it look like I am on top of my game; I know what I am doing and I keep to my words. People love and appreciate that.

My belief about being truthful is when people trust you; they will refer and recommend you to others over and over again. There is nothing better than when people can trust you with their time, resources and projects.

In whatever thing you do, be truthful. Say things you mean and stick with them. Don't cook up stories to look better or feel better about anything you do. People may not know at first, if they eventually find out, it will ruin your credibility and chances to work with them further.

Transparency is key in whatever thing you do be it friendship or business. Be truthful at all times.

ACKNOWLEDGEMENT

Taking the time to acknowledge people is another important thing that will help you on your entrepreneur journey.

When people contact you whether by mail, telephone calls, or text messages, it is very important to acknowledge them. Don't wait till too late to respond to their questions or messages or requests. If you do that, it sends the message that you take people for granted and they are not worthy of your time.

If complaints come to you about anything, acknowledge those too by responding and assuring the people you are dealing with that you are sorry and that you will fix or take care of their complaint. When you give them your words, ensure to follow through to the end. Sort out the problem, follow through and ensure they are happy because they deserve to get the best from you especially if they have paid for the service.

Acknowledgement is not only for those who pay for the service you offer. It is also important to acknowledge people who support you, celebrate you, inspire you, motivate you, and just cheer you on to do better and to be better.

Acknowledgment and trust go a long way in building a long-term relationship in any thing you do.

GRATITUDE

Being grateful is one of the best life philosophies to live by. I have had so many successful people talk about being grateful and how they show gratitude to God even if it seems like they are failing.

Being grateful when things are not going right is very scriptural. Phil 4:6 says, "Do not worry about anything; instead, pray about everything. Tell God what you need and thank him for what he has done." When you have the heart of gratitude, you will more or less be distracted from the things that seem like problems to you and you will continue to focus more and more on the things that make you happy.

The same way you relate with God with a heart of gratitude is the same way you should relate with people who help or do things for you. No matter how small the gift or the gesture, always make sure to show appreciation. Be grateful for people's time by acknowledging what they have done. Let them know how grateful you are by saying thank you. Being grateful distracts you from feeling sorry for yourself or from being weary and helps you focus on the Father who knows and can do all things in his time.

OFFENCES

No matter what you do or where you are from, it is impossible to expect that people won't offend you at times. It is also possible that people may find offence with how you do things from time to time. Offending and being offended is unfortunately part of life. It is best not to be surprised by it, instead be humble and quickly take action if you offend someone by apologising. No one is perfect so don't expect yourself or anyone else to be perfect.

When people offend you, it is important to let them know. If they apologise, let it go by forgiving them and let that be the end of it. When you offend people and they let you know, apologise to them and let that be the end of it. Having said that, it is possible that not everyone will be happy with you for one reason or the other. Once you have acknowledged you are wrong and have apologized, walk away and so be it. There is no need to waste time or dwell on things that are unnecessary like offences. Remember your time is precious, don't waste it on offences.

BE HUMBLE

Philippians 2:8 says, "And being found in appearance as a man, He humbled Himself and became obedient to *the point of* death, even the death of the cross. [9] Therefore God also has highly exalted Him and given Him the name which is above every name." The reward of humility is submission and honour. When you are humble you are exalted and respected. Be humble and you will be exalted just as God exalted his son Jesus. You can never demand respect; you earn or command it. When you are humble, you are setting yourself up to be rewarded with respect and honour. Do not let success turn you to an arrogant person. Respect people and in return God will honour you.

KINDNESS

Being kind is a great character to have. One of the fruits of the spirit according to Galatians 5:22-23, is to be kind. Being kind is a commandment, so no matter who you meet, who they are, what you think they are worth, or what they can offer you, be kind to everyone.

Sometimes when people go through things, they tend to go away from others or separate themselves so they can reflect and get their act together. If they come by you, they may seem hostile or they may seem unkind because of what they are going through. What you owe them is kindness, be kind to them especially if you know they are going through a hard time.

Being nice now is different from being kind. Someone may be nice to you because of what they could benefit from you. Be careful not to mix being nice with being kind. Be kind to people but don't let anyone take advantage of you by being nice because of what they hope to benefit.

If you come by anyone who seem weary, broken, sad, or discouraged, don't overlook him or her and don't just conclude they will be fine. Your help or your word of courage to them may be of enormous help to cheer them up and help them get out of their troubles. When you are kind to people going through tough times or issues of life, they will never forget you when eventually they get better and they are themselves again.

This may sound like a broken record but when you are facing challenges yourself and you still show love or reach out to others who may be facing challenges, you will be surprised at the strength you will build to find your way out of your own challenge. Trouble may last for a night but joy will definitely come in the morning. Kindness is a great attitude or character to build.

IGNORE HATERS & CRITICISM

In my line of work, I come in contact with so many people from all parts of the world. So many of them have been extremely kind to me and very supportive. Having said that, I have also come by haters. They come on me with full force.

What I do is simply ignore them. When they leave me hurtful comments, I read through, leave it for a moment and come back to it again. If there is anything to learn from their criticism, I take it on board, if not; I ignore such comments and stay focused on the positives.

Learn to ignore haters. You do not owe them any explanations of what you are doing and how you do them. Responding to haters is a waste of time and energy. Haters do not deserve your time.

As for Criticism, the hobby of some people is to criticize everything and anything. They criticize even the best of things. It is important to focus on taking criticism that is constructive and not ones meant intentionally for malicious reasons.

Be careful who you accept criticism from, the people who don't create anything or understand what you do won't be able to relate to what you do. They may not be people to take criticism from. For such people, a thank you so much will be ideal and then move on. However, learn from your critics, especially if they are a customer or prospect so that you can learn and improve on your creation or services.

BE PASSIONATE

This last character trait I want to share with you is imperative. It is one that can determine how far you will go in making money. It takes time, effort, and so much work to build a reputable brand but in a twinkle of an eye, everything could be gone. For this reason, it is important to be truly passionate about what you do. Do not allow your passion for what you do to only show when you are making money. It is the passion you have that will drive your brand whether you are making money in that moment or not.

While it is important to sell your products or services, it is more important to sell yourself. When you share what you are passionate about with passion and the reason why you do what you do, people buy into what you stand for even more than what you really sell. People buy your determination, they buy your passion, they buy your presence and they then buy what you sell or offer. In simple words, people buy YOU first before they buy your products or services.

Now do this simple exercise in your "gift book":

- Which of the character traits above do you think you need to build on? Be intentional about working at them.

Well done to you, you are doing awesome.

CHAPTER 23

DRESS TO WIN

"I like dressing good. Makes you feel confident. Sort of like self-confident. Sort of like self-expression kind of thing to me; mostly, I like to dress classy; it looks better, cleaner and makes me feel good." ~Rory MacDonald

From my experience in Fashion and HR, whether you like it or not, people will address you the way you are dressed. The fact remains that before you open your mouth to speak, people see how you look first. It is always best to look well at all times. It leaves a lasting impression.

When you dress well, you feel confident. When you are confident in the way you look, you carry yourself confidently. When you carry yourself confidently, you speak confidently. When you are confident in the way you speak, people listen and buy into you and most likely buy what you have to offer.

Research shows that successful people dress well. I will be surprised if this is otherwise. If you have ever gone for an interview, you may have noticed that your look plays a very important role in the way your interviewer sees you. A minimum of 7% of the total interview score is what you earn when you dress well to an interview. That interview rule comes to play in the business world as well, when people see you are dressed well; they tend to take you more seriously. I believe very much in favour but I know your look play a very important role in how people perceive you. And why wait for people's perception of you to dress well, dress well anyway because you deserve it.

To move your business from just a potential to purpose, you must begin to dress well. You must dress well at all times so when you have the opportunity to talk about what you do, you will not miss out on the chance to do it because you are not well dressed.

As an entrepreneur, it is important to dress well because people also "size you up" based on how you are dressed and they want to pay you based on that even if you can offer more. In simple terms, your look can make or break how much you get paid especially in the creative world. If you dress well, people offer you more and if you dress poorly, they offer you less pay.

Also, know the kind of dressing that works for your line of business. If you do presentations or proposals in the corporate world, you should dress formal or semi-formal depending on how they dress in that organisation. If your line of business permits you to dress down or casual, it is best to dress casual but ensure you are well put together and neat. If you are not sure what to wear to any occasion, do your research or ask a Stylist. This is part of what I help my clients figure out.

Here's 7 reasons why it is important to dress well at all times, especially when you are moving your gift from just a hobby into a career or business:

1. It makes a good impression: People notice you when you dress well and dressing well makes you presentable.
2. Confidence: Getting a simple compliment about how you look can actually boost your confidence. A compliment can also turn a bad mood into a good one.
3. You want to make the most of every opportunity: You never know who you will run into!
4. Self-Expression: You can express yourself in the way you dress.
5. When you look good, you keep moving and are more productive: If you are working from home on your gift, wearing decent clothes even while working from home actually helps you to be more productive. Instead of staying in your pyjamas, wear something presentable and comfy that can inspire you to sit by your desk to get some work done. Staying in your pyjamas all day may give you a go-back-to-bed idea; this is bad for productivity.
6. You deserve to feel fabulous: Don't wait for only special occasions to dress well. Dress well all the time. Dressing well is not about how much you pay for your clothes; it is all about being presentable, clean, neat and well put together.
7. Dressing well helps you stand out: You look great and stand out compared to those who do not try at all: It is very important to dress well as an entrepreneur. When you do, people take you very seriously and are likely to listen to you compared to when you do not try.

Dressing well is not rocket science. It is something you shouldn't have to worry too much about so you can focus on what is more important which is the job at hand.

To dress well, try this simple approach:

Invest in key pieces.

A wardrobe is not all about how many clothes but how well you wear them.

For Men, you need these wardrobe essentials: a fitted blazer, a well fitted trouser, a couple of button down shirts, a tie, a pair of jeans, a pair of shoes that fit well, a pair of slacks or casual pants, a couple of tee shirts, a pair of sneakers, depending on the weather where you live, an outer wear or a coat that fits well and accessories like cufflinks, bow tie and pocket tissue. You can also include a brief case to your list of accessories for when you start attending meetings to hold your paper work.

Other things you need to help you look good underneath:

Inner wear (singlet or v-neck tee), boxers and briefs. To look well groomed, get clippers, shaving sticks, deodorant / perfume.

For Ladies, you need these wardrobe essentials: a fitted blazer, a fitted skirt, a couple of fitted shirts or blouses, a little black dress or shirt dress, a pair of well-fitted jeans, a pair of well-fitted heels or flats, a couple of basic tee shirts, depending on your weather: an outerwear or a coat that fits well and accessories like a structured bag to help hold your essentials, brooches, scarves, a pair of stud earrings like pearls, statement necklaces and sunglasses (optional)

Other things you need to help you look good underneath:

At least two fitted bras; a basic one and a lingerie, pants; choose whichever design you like, a pair of spanx or anything similar; this is always handy to help you accentuate your shape. To look well groomed, you need your hair to be well done and neat whether your hair is natural or permed, a red lipstick is always a good idea for "glam up day", get Vaseline to keep your lips well moisturized, a lip gloss is good if you don't wear lipsticks, you need deodorant to keep dry and perfume to smell extra good.

That is a quick summary of what you need to dress well, look great, and remain presentable once you are ready to go from potential to fulfill purpose. Like I always say, image is everything.

If the advertisement of a product appeals to you, you are likely to buy it but if it doesn't, you just won't feel the need to buy it. Make yourself appealing always.

1. Plan Outfits ahead:

Rushing out means you always have to throw on anything you find. So to always look well put together, always plan outfit ahead of time.

2. Repeat Your Outfits:

A lot of people have this mindset that you cannot repeat an outfit. In my humble opinion, it is okay to repeat an outfit. It is how you wear the outfit that matters. Change of accessories or change of shoes will modify a look and will make it look different. This approach works all the time!

Now grab your "gift book" and do this simple exercise:

- Do you present yourself in a presentable way or do you think you just can't be bothered about the way you look?
- Now write down three ways you want to be intentional about your look.

Don't forget, image is everything. Always present yourself the way you want to be addressed.

IMPORTANT NOTE!

In the next chapter, I have a very special and heartfelt note to women like me. Dear women, please read.

After that note to women, I have prayers for you dear readers and my send off and well wishes to you.

Please keep reading.

CHAPTER 24

DEAR WOMAN LIKE ME

Dear woman like me; this is my special note to you. Please insert your name below and repeat the next few lines after me:

My name is ________________________ and I am a woman!

I am a woman first before I am a wife. I am a woman first before I am a mother. I am a woman and my identity is found in God because I am special to him and He loves me.

My job does not define me, my career does not define me, my children do not define me, and my husband does not define me. I am a woman who has a vision, dreams, and aspirations; I am a woman and I know who I am.

I am a woman who loves and cares and because I love and care, I love my family and friends; I love my husband in submission to him; I love my children and guide them according to God's instructions. I am a woman!

How does it feel to say those lines? Did you feel confident saying them or do you have doubt in your mind while saying them? Do you know who you are? Do you feel like you may have lost yourself because you care for everyone else but yourself? Do you really feel like a woman? One who has dreams, aspirations, goals, ambition and one who cares for herself? How do you really feel? Are you angry about what you didn't do? Are you blaming yourself for what you could have done? Are you angry because you gave up your career since you had your children? Are you lost in the world of your husband and children? What is it?

Please answer all of those questions truthfully so you can determine where you are in life now and where you truthfully want to be. When you answer those questions, ask yourself why you are not where you desire to be? Why have you taken the back seat and how can you begin to make yourself a priority too, just as you do for your husband and children?

Be sincere with yourself and answer those questions because you cannot afford to waste away on the inside with doubt and resentment while being a mother and a wife. You can impact your generation by the potentials and gift you have inside of you. Now it is time to prayerfully unlock them and it is time to begin to walk in your purpose. Don't think you can't because you can.

It is possible that the enemy is saying that it is too late for you to do anything because you are of a certain age, but don't believe that. Believe what God says about you. Believe what God has laid in your heart to do and believe that with His help you can achieve everything you set your mind to do.

Dear woman, I need you to read chapters 3, 4 and 7 of this book again very carefully and begin to unlock all those possibilities you have inside of you. From now on, begin to live intentionally and deliberately, stop wasting time, stop blaming others for what you didn't do, and focus on what you can do so you can achieve more.

From today forward, care for yourself, your family and everyone else who depends on you with confidence while fulfilling your purpose. God will give you the grace to do what you need to do and to use your gifts in some special way. It is time dear woman, to get up from the back seat and walk alongside your husband and children holding your head high, knowing you were made for a purpose and you can fulfill that purpose.

A WOMAN'S SEASON

Even though in all our lives, there are many seasons. In a woman's life especially, there are many seasons. One season of a woman's life is when she is young, unmarried, with a lot of potential ahead of her. A job or business, could be part of that too depending on the path the woman has chosen to follow.

Another season for many women is when she falls in love and then gets married. Another for many women is when she has her first child; another is when she has more children. And these seasons keep changing. Even if you do not choose to marry or have children, you may go into busier seasons in your career or seasons where you care for aging parents or when you are needed more by friends or family members.

While the seasons of your life may change, your goals, desires, and hopes can remain vibrant. The dream you have for yourself doesn't have to change because you are caring for your family. You can have it all; a good home, a good career, a good job, and Godly children. You can have it all but it may not all happen at the same time. Keep believing for and working toward these dreams and desires that were planted inside of you. Quit thinking of the deceits and the lies of the enemy that says you can't, because you can.

For you as a woman to live a stress free, fulfilled, and purposeful life you must pay attention to all the seasons of your life and embrace them. When you embrace the season you are in, you will be surprised at how fulfilling, stress free, and productive your life can be. And as you take care of every other person, do not forget to take care of you too. Your schedule may be tight because you have to do this and that, but never let your schedule be too tight to accommodate your needs too. Caring for your family is important but caring for yourself is as important.

Ephesians 3:8 instructs that there is a time for everything. There is indeed time for everything under heaven. As a woman, you have to be willing to study and accept the time you are in so you can create that routine that can accommodate everything including yourself. Dear woman, it is very important to embrace the season you are in and enjoy that season. Please note, for all the seasons of your life, God is with you. Please recognize that and enjoy it. Don't be in a hurry for the next season of your life, live in the moment and enjoy the now.

While it is okay to think broadly or deeply on all of those things you want to achieve in your life as a woman, it is also important to recognize with the help of God, the season you are in. When you recognize the season you are in, you work your God-given purpose effortlessly and you achieve what you desire to achieve.

Like I said above, when you get married and have children, you are in a new season of life. That may not be the time to travel as much as you used to when you had only yourself to be concerned with. That may not be the time to take on a new role in another city. That may not be the time to start another project.

While it is important to recognize the season you are in, you must also understand and believe that you can achieve and do all you want to do as a wife and as a mother. You can fulfill your God-given purpose. The only catch is to recognize what to do and at what time to do it. With the help of God, you can do all the things you want to do once you know the season you are in.

I remember at some stage in my life when my children were very young. Let me be precise here, Sammy my younger son was about 2 years old and Daniel was about 4 years at that time. I would leave them at the crèche (nursery/sitter) from about 7am till about 6pm to go to my job at the bank. That wasn't bad to do at all; all it took out of my purse was money to pay the crèche, which was quite a lot, but it was worth it.

When Daniel my older son got into junior infant, my routine changed because both of them couldn't be at the crèche anymore. Sammy would go to the crèche and Daniel to primary school. I made arrangements for Daniel to be collected after school with friends whose children went to the same school as him. It didn't take long before the arrangement failed.

To avoid panic and lack of concentration in my job, I quickly had to readjust my schedule and planned around my children so I could take care of them and take care of my career and myself at the same time. It took a while for me to get it right but once I was at peace within me of the season I was in, I didn't find it hard to adjust my lifestyle to accommodate my family, my job, my home, and every other thing. As I embraced the season, I enjoyed everything that season brought; my life as it was, the children, the job, and every other thing in between.

You may be wondering where my husband was at this stage because I didn't mention him in this picture. My husband at this point lived and worked in an entirely different continent. He had his business in Nigeria so at the time he lived in Nigeria but visited often to spend time with us. Whenever he was around, my life was a bit easier because he would help with everything. Aside from having to be gone so much for work, he didn't fail in his duties as a husband and as a father. He provided for the children and me both physically, financially, emotionally, and spiritually. Never was there a time when he shifted his responsibilities to me.

Dear women like me; you are not competing with anyone. After your father in heaven, your family should come first before any career. If everything fails, the only thing that could be standing with you with the help of God will be your family. What this means is, if you lose your job just like I did at some stage in my life, you can change jobs. You can also change jobs if the one you are in does not suit your lifestyle anymore. But it will be hard to change your beloved family if you truly love them.

Recognizing the season you are in and embracing it as a woman gives you liberty, less stress, and a balanced life to do all you are destined to do. Whatever it is you have set your mind to do, you can do. Know the season you are in, embrace it, and be thankful for where you are. When you are thankful for now, you see beyond the now; you see a future that is bright and a woman who can fulfill purpose by doing what she loves.

Grab your "gift book" and answer these questions:

- Where are you now and what season are you in?
- What can you do to help yourself develop those goals you have swept under the rug because you are caring for your husband and children?
- What can you do now to move you forward? Write down the steps you can take to achieve them? Please take your time to do this exercise and when you finish, be mindful to follow through.
- Dear woman, may I request that you read this chapter again please?

Thank you, you did so amazing.

GET TO KNOW YOURSELF

I hear of the saying that women don't support women. While this may be a casual saying, I do believe that women who have the mentality of not supporting others are the ones who don't know themselves. A woman who knows herself and what she stands for would not have any reason not to support another woman. A woman who knows herself supports everyone including every woman that crosses her path.

A woman who knows herself would have real friends and relationships that could last a lifetime. She would have people in her life that if anything goes wrong whether in her home, her job, or her business, she can talk to them about how to figure out a lasting solution for the problem.

A woman who knows herself is not seeking other people's approval before she goes for what she wants. If she wants something, she prayerfully goes for it and commits to it in full until she gets the results she wants.

A woman's who know herself doesn't want to be who she is not or starts doing what she is not called to do. A woman who knows herself walks in her purpose and do everything to be a better version of herself and not someone else.

YOUR RELATIONSHIP WITH YOU FIRST

The one thing I am sure of about a lot of women is that women are caring. These are the women who have that little tenderness in their hearts for their friends, family, children, and co-workers, etc.

While it is really important to have that tender heart, meekness, and gentleness in the spirit, it is also important not to forget to love yourself and take care of yourself too. As a woman, it is important to have a solid relationship with yourself, know yourself, and understand yourself so you can be who you want to be. When you have a thorough relationship with yourself, it will not be too hard to know if you are being exploited, bullied, taken advantage of, or cheated.

It is okay to be meek, soft-spoken, and gentle but be aware of who you are and what you stand for so that you will not be pushed around. There is this saying that says, "If you stand for nothing, you fall for anything". Know who you are and what you stand for as a woman so you are not pushed around by the people you help, the people you work with, and the people you live with.

KNOWING YOURSELF AT HOME

When you have a relationship with yourself, you feel confident at home to run your home with wisdom. If you are a wife, God's instruction to you is for you to submit to your husband according to Ephesians 5:22. Yes, it is important to submit to your husband, he is your partner and lover. When you submit to him, his obligation is for him to love you according to Ephesians 5:23. You are partners with your husband and not rivals. You are his helpmate and he is yours. You are a team.

A woman who knows herself knows the difference between being loved and being abused. It is important to give in submission and also to receive by letting your husband love you. Don't try to do everything yourself. Allow your husband, your partner and soul mate, to love you. In loving, he gives you his love, heart, time, possessions, support and everything he has. Do not hesitate to do the same in submission.

It is not impossible as a woman to be more knowledgeable, more intelligent, and more spiritually sound than your husband. It is also not impossible that you have a bigger career or business than your husband. If this is the case, still in submission, help your husband prayerfully to achieve or attain the standard or position you think he can attain. If your husband is all of the above and you are not, in submission, he will help you achieve your goals and lift you up.

Don't nag, instead pray more and don't wish, instead act more and you will achieve more.

A woman who knows herself will not be in competition with her husband or become arrogant because she is doing better. Instead she would pray with and for him and together they can both be who God has called them to be. Don't try to figure everything on your own, let God be at the centre of everything and He will take care of you because truly He loves you.

KNOWING YOURSELF AT WORK

In a professional setting and in so many other works of life, men dominate because that is what the society expects and permits. While there are more male bosses than there are female bosses, it is important to learn to express yourself. Be sure to let your voice be heard if you have any concerns.

The thing about not asking is that you already have a no for an answer. If you need flexibility in your job, ask. If you believe you need a pay raise as your male colleague received, just ask. If you need time off to take care of your home or family, ask. If you know yourself enough and understand what you stand for, you will not have difficulty in asking for anything you think you deserve. The people in higher position than you or your bosses are human like you. Why take a chance by not asking? Remember not asking is an automatic NO, so learn to ask.

As a working woman also, work diligently, be punctual, and continue to learn more or study more so you can show yourself approved. If you want that promotion or you want that pay raise, prayerfully and strategically dedicate time to your goal. By committing to do what you are supposed to do, you are that much closer to getting what you deserve.

Dear woman like me, you can have it all. From now on, be intentional about having a relationship with yourself and setting goals so you can achieve them. Every other person does not define you. Love your family but never put yourself last. Someday, your children will be gone away from home and you will be left with what you didn't do. So this does not happen, begin to take action now to care for yourself, love yourself, and also begin to work towards achieving those goals you have always wanted to achieve. When you do these things, you will feel fulfilled and God will be glorified through you. You can have it all in His perfect timing as you use your gifts to fulfill your purpose.

TO THE YOUNG WOMEN IN THIS AGE

Congratulations you have been born in an era where there are so many advocates for women. An era where there could be a first female president of the United States of America. An era, where there are a lot of women, groups, societies, bodies, and institutions fighting for the right of the women and girls both at home and at work. All of these are very good but the most important thing for you as a young woman is to love yourself; love your body, love your skin, and prayerfully know **why** God created you and what He wants you to be.

If you know who you are as a young woman and you know what you want, you will save yourself the hassle of letting another person define you. An example of letting another define you is falling in the hands of an abusive or violent boyfriend. Do not start your life enduring pain or abuse from any man in the name of love. A man who loves you will never hit, bully, or abuse you in the name of love; instead he will respect you and your decisions, support you, and pray for/ with you.

As a young lady, you must be able to stand and to say stop to anything, anybody, or any situation that looks abusive. Know yourself, study, get education or training, and prepare yourself for a bright future that is ahead of you.

As a young woman, it is important for you to have people you look up to. The best people you can look up to are your parents if they are good examples for you. If not, you must be willing to find role models who can inspire, direct, encourage, and mentor you to be who you want to be. It is okay to seek a mentor but be sure to choose a mentor who can listen more than they talk and one who can give you Godly counsel.

You could be growing up in an environment where abuse is the order of the day. If this is the case, be intentional about how you want to live and make up your mind that as you grow, you will not fall into the same cycle. Break that chain of modern day slavery and abuse, and instead embrace the love of God so you can be who you want to be.

I love digging into the success stories of successful people to see what I can learn from them. Recently, I watched some of Oprah's stories on her Oprah Winfrey Network (OWN). In that story, she said she lived with and was raised by her grandmother. Her grandmother worked as a slave. She said whenever her grand mother did laundry and was putting them on the line to dry, she would call her and give her instructions on how she can be confident at doing laundry so when she gets older to go work as a slave, she would do it effortlessly. Oprah said even though her grandmother's hope and desire for her was to be a slave because she didn't know different, she said, that wasn't her desire for herself. She said she knew she wasn't going to be a slave and neither was she going to settle for less. She had the drive and determination. She said she believed there was a force greater than her leading her; she said that force was God. She knew what she wanted and despite all odds she is who she is today. Oprah is who she is today because of self will, determination, and because she refused to settle for less.

Dear young women, what anyone says or thinks of you does not define you. The expectations of others won't determine where or who you will be. Your determination, zeal, works with God and your desires can make you be who you want to be. Please don't settle for less. You can do great things, greater than Oprah or what any other person in history has ever done. You can do it, it starts with self believe and how you see yourself.

SELF CARE

So many women let themselves go once they become mums. Some women let go of their bodies, their careers, and forget who they really are and the ambition they had before becoming mums.

It is okay to love your husband, your children, and ensure that your home is safe and happy but it is even more important to take care of yourself just like you do for your family.

It is evident that your body changes when you have children. While I am a believer of loving your body the way you want. It is important to take care of your body. If you are not happy with the changes that has occurred in your body after you have children, don't let go, take care of that body and get it right in your own way, not what the society expects. Do what you can to get your body to where you are pleased, not to try to make others happy.

Take care of your body, take care of your soul, and take care of your spirit. Exercise so you can be fit to run your home. Eat healthy so you can feel well and be strong enough to reach your goals and take care of your family. Take care of you first so that you can also take care of others.

Get your hair done, do your nails; they don't have to be polished or painted but keep them clean. Dress well, look put together, and live well. You owe it to yourself to take care of you.

Taking care of you is not selfish and neither is it carnal. It is your gift to yourself because you deserve it. Also don't forget that young woman that man feel in love with before she became a mum. Pay attention to you so you can remain youthful and beautiful to your man.

Self-care is way more than physical. Take care of yourself by investing in profitable things. Buy and read a book or books. Learn a new skill. Take a new course. Volunteer in the society to teach what you know; it brings a sense of fulfillment and achievement.

Self-care also branches out to the spiritual. Know the Word and the promises God has for you so you can live a fulfilled life. This out of everything I mentioned in self-care is the most important. When you get this right, you will be surprised that every other thing will follow and fall in place.

It is important as a woman not to be on the bottom of your list in your life. Your family is very important and God planted you in your family because he knows you can take care of that family. Even as God has trusted you with your family, He has also given you visions, aspirations and dreams that you can fulfill only if you do not put yourself at the bottom of the list in your life. Take care of your family; your husband and your children but ensure to take good care of you.

Dear women like me, take a moment to ask yourself these questions. You can answer them in your gift book:

- Who are you? Do you know yourself? What is your identity tied to?
- Are you caring for yourself just like you are caring for your family?
- Are you putting yourself last and belittling your gift and potentials?
- What do you want to achieve and how can you achieve those things?

Answer these questions honestly and truthfully. Once you do, write a few ways or action plan you can care for yourself and improve yourself down. Then begin to work towards achieving your set goals.

My prayer for you is that God will help and strengthen you to live the fulfilled life He has called you to.

CHAPTER 25

WHERE ARE YOU NOW?

Have you made the decision to start using your gift now or are you still unsure on how to go about it? Honestly, the journey of using your gift may not be the easiest of things to do especially when you have a busy lifestyle. However, by grace, you can do it, so all the potential you carry inside can be unlocked and they can become a purpose.

I hope from now onwards, you can begin to take a little step each day towards that big dream you've always wanted to achieve and in no time, you will be able to achieve that big goal of yours. Taking a small step is better than not moving at all. So whatever your own gift is, embrace them, own them and use them to fulfill specific purpose for your life.

With the help of God, recognise when you have to crawl and when you have to stand, then know when you have to walk, and then when it is time to run, start running and when it is time to jump, just do it and you will be surprised at what you can do.

I recently saw the quote of the day on the Forbes website and the quote was by Bruce Lee. He says and I quote "Always be yourself, don't go outside and look for a successful person and duplicate it".

What that quote is saying is; when you start using what you have or your gift, do it your own way. Don't copy anyone or try to be what you are not or walk in someone else's purpose. I encourage you to let God help you and you will be surprised at what you can do with his help. You are worth much more than you even know. God has created you for a special purpose. Please don't let it remain a potential forever but do all you can to fulfill that purpose for your life.

I am looking forward by faith to fulfill my own purpose in life so God can be glorified through me. For now, I am thankful for where God has brought me from and what He is doing right now in my life. I am also prayerfully looking forward to everything He has planned for me for the future.

Since I made up my mind to start using what I have from my tiny home office in Ireland, I have confidently turned my gift into a thriving career and have become a mentor to many. Most importantly, I was able to rescue a girl who lives all the way in West Virginia from committing suicide just by making encouraging videos. Just by making videos! Isn't that amazing that God would use me in such a powerful way?

He can do that and so much more with your own gift too if you will let Him. Your gift could position you in a place where you can help, serve, impact, and inspire so many people from all around the world. Your gift can make a way for you only if you follow through. Please don't waste it, do whatever you can to fulfill your purpose by using your gifts.

MY PRAYER FOR YOU

Dear God, I know that all good gifts are from you and you have gifted each and every one reading this according to your great purpose. I pray for as many as are still confused or are unsure of their gift to get clarity right now. I pray that you give them the confidence to discover and recognize their gifts, embrace them and own them. I pray that you give them the wisdom to manage their time well and the strength to build on and develop their gifts. I pray for favour for them in your sight and in the sight of everyone who comes their way as they use their gifts. I pray that you will connect them to their destiny helpers. I pray you help them turn all their potential into fulfilled purpose for their lives and your name be glorified in Jesus name. Amen.

CONCLUSION & MY BEST WISHES

I wish I could meet each of you who has journeyed through my book. I'd love to chat with you and have fun going through your style to help you find your signature look that makes you feel confident as you fulfill your purpose. But I know this is not possible. So I leave you with my prayer and best wishes as you go and use your gifts, taking them from potential to fulfill purpose.

I encourage you to be confident as you study God's promises for your life. Write them out in your "gift book" and put your name in the verses to remind you that they are yours! God speaks life through his words over each and every one of us but we must claim them and believe them for it to have power in our lives. Will you be brave and believe that it applies to YOUR life? I hope so.

Finally, I leave you with this great promise from God from Jeremiah 29 vs 11 which says: For I know the thoughts that I think toward you, saith the LORD, thoughts of peace, and not of evil, to give you an expected end.

Now go confidently and take your gifts from potential to fulfill purpose. Yes, you can!

NOTE FROM AUTHOR

I do hope you have been richly blessed by this book and I am more than excited to think of all you will accomplish when you take the bold step to start using what you have or your God-given gifts.

If you have been blessed by this book, please:

Recommend it: it will be a great honour to me if you would tell at least one person about this book. Please share it with your friends and family, it will bless them richly.

Tweet it: please tweet about it by using the #usewhatyouhave.

Review it: please leave a review of the book on Amazon. You can also review the book on your blog if you review books.

If you want more copies or bulk copies of this book, please send me an email on mojintouch@gmail.com. You can also buy the book directly from Amazon.

It will also be a great honour to me to hear from you and how this book has helped or encouraged you. I am everywhere online; please connect with me on:

Facebook: www.facebook.com/mojintouch

Twitter: www.twitter.com/mojintouch

Instagram: www.instagram.com/mojintouch

Email: mojintouch@gmail.com or mojisola@mojintouch.com

Website: www.mojintouch.com

Youtube: www.youtube.com/c/mojintouch

If you would like me to speak or have a book reading at your event or programme, please contact me on info@mojintouch.com.

If you need personal styling or image consultation or need some encouragement on how you can take your gifts from potential to fulfill purpose, please contact me on info@mojintouch.com

About The Author

Mojisola Obazuaye is a writer, speaker, stylist and YouTube creator. She is a Christian and a passionate believer that everybody **MUST** find and fulfill their purpose in life. Out of her passion, she created the Moj In Touch blog (www.mojintouch.com) where she inspires, motivates, encourages and mentors others on finding & fulfilling their purpose. She also helps clients create digital contents; strategise campaign to maximise their online presence and serves as image coach to several clients and her blog readers from all around the world.

She has a first degree in Microbiology from the University of Ibadan, Nigeria and her second degree in Industrial Biology with

Bioinformatics from the Institute of Technology, Carlow, Ireland. Although she has her educational background in science, she only worked a few years in the science field but has more than 10 years experience in banking, customer relations and human relations. She is also a Qualified Image Consultant.

She is a frequent speaker at business events and non-profit organisations. She has presented at different conferences including "Girls Arize", a seminar for the empowerment of the girl child amongst many others. On her speaking engagements, she has presented on finding and fulfilling purpose, profit from blogging, self-development, empowerment of women and girls, healthy living and body confidence.

She was nominated for the Irish Blogs Awards in 2015 and was selected to be a part of the 2016 YouTube Creators Day at the Google Headquarters in Dublin. Her work has been featured on the Guardian (Nigeria), Fashion & Style Police (UK) and Style-Motivation (USA), amongst many others.

She is married to Efe and they have 2 darling sons.

Your Personal Notes and Work Book

Your Personal Notes and Work Book

Your Personal Notes and Work Book